Computers for people

Computers
for
people

Jerry Willis and Merl Miller

dilithium Press
Beaverton, Oregon

Throughout this book, the use of ® or ™ indicates a trademark of Atari, Inc., unless otherwise footnoted.

ISBN: 0-918398-64-9
Library of Congress catalog card number: 81-69979

Printed in the United States of America.

dilithium Press
P.O. Box 606
Beaverton, Oregon 97075

Acknowledgements

One of the most difficult things to do, is write a book under a very tight deadline. This book would not have been possible without the help of some special people; our thanks to Sally Bowman of Atari, Inc., Patti Miller and Debbie Willis. Especial thanks to one of our favorite computer dealers, Jerry Scott, Sounds, Etc., Watonga, Oklahoma.

Jerry Willis
Merl Miller

Contents

CHAPTER 1 **Computers Aren't Scary Anymore** 1

CHAPTER 2 **How To Buy Your Own Computer** 11

CHAPTER 3 **Home, Home on the Computer (Where the RAM and the ROM Roam)** . . 25

CHAPTER 4 **Shopping For A Computer For Your Home** 39

CHAPTER 5 **The Outer Limits: Communicating With the World** 47

CHAPTER 6 **Buying A Communications Computer** . 61

CHAPTER 7 **The Teaching Machine** 71

CHAPTER 8 **Selecting an Educational Computer** 89

CHAPTER 9 **Solving Business and Professional Problems** 99

CHAPTER 10 **Investing In A Computer For Your Business** 117

CHAPTER 11 **The Stuff That Makes It Happen: Software** 125

CHAPTER 12 **It's Not Magic: The Basic Computer™** . . . 133

CHAPTER 13 **The Current Crop** 145

CHAPTER 14 **Where To Find Everything We Didn't Tell You** 161

Glossary 173

Index 189

Chapter 1

Computers Aren't Scary Anymore

One of the biggest problems most people face in dealing with computers is fear. We've been taught to think of computers as big, complicated machines that, in the wrong hands, can do terrible things. We've been told for many years that the reason the bill was wrong was because the computer made a mistake. In reality, what happened was a human made a mistake and blamed it on the computer. The computer is just like any other machine or tool. It is only as good as the person who runs it and only as useful as you make it. You can choose to use it in any manner you want. It won't take over your life, run off with your spouse, or cause you strife. It does only what you tell it to do.

If you don't want to learn anything beyond how to load a program into the machine and run it, you don't have to. You don't need to know how to program in a *computer language.* In fact you don't have to know anymore about your computer than you do about your car. There are thousands of professionally prepared programs available. These *canned* programs cover a wide variety of subjects. Here are a few examples:

Educational Programs. These programs can help teach a grade schooler all of the states and capitals or show an adult how a nuclear power plant works.

Personal Enrichment. You can chart your biorhythms or play the stock market.

Game Programs. You can zap invaders from space with laser rays or play chess.

Business Programs. There are programs for inventory control, accounts receivable, word processing and much more.

Arts Programs. You can paint abstract pictures on a video canvas or create the great American opera with a computer-controlled music composing program.

The five areas mentioned above, as well as many others, will be discussed in detail in the following chapters. Remember, a computer is a tool. How you use this fantastic tool is up to you.

A computer has a lot of flexibility. It will do the same things a calculator will do (e.g. balance your checkbook), and it will do many more routine clerical jobs such as keeping track of Aunt Edna's birthday. It will also do some very innovative jobs. For example, one of the most innovative programs we've heard about is one that keeps track of a three-year-old diabetic. It tells his parents when they should give him insulin, what his reaction to the insulin is, and how he is doing in general. The computer not only displays his current vital signs numerically, it also creates a graph which shows the trend across several days and weeks. The important thing about all of this is that the child's parents are just ordinary folks like you and I. Neither parent has any medical background or college training in computers. They bought their computer and taught themselves enough to create a modern miracle for their son. Take a minute to think about it. How could you use a computer to improve your life?

You might even want to learn how to program your computer. It's not as difficult as most people think. For instance, here is a simple program that adds two numbers:

```
10 A = 2
20 B = 3
30 PRINT A + B
```

If you really want to see how a computer works, you can run this one on an ATARI® 800™ Computer or an ATARI® 400™ Computer. Tell your ATARI Home Computer retailer that you would like to run a BASIC program. After your retailer has the computer ready, type in the program exactly as shown. Press the return key after each line. After you have entered line 30, type Run. The computer will immediately display 5. You knew all along that this was the answer, so what does this prove? Well, for one thing it proves that the computer is just a dumb machine that does what you tell it. You also learned that you can figure out what a computer program will tell the computer to do.

If you can figure out what a computer program does, then you can change it to fit your needs. There are a lot of things you can do with this simple program. For instance, you can tell it to ask you for the values of A and B. Then, you can enter any two numbers you want and it will faithfully add them up for you. If you wanted to, you could have it subtract, multiply or divide the numbers. Ask your retailer to show you how. You'll be surprised at how easy it is. You may even want to learn a little programming. This is one of the really nice things about computers, you can either learn a little or a lot and still get a lot out of your computer.

Perhaps you want to use your computer in your business. It can be used as both accountant and assistant manager. It can help you do your job better. Thousands of small businesses use computers. Managers, doctors, lawyers, dentists and other professionals are also discovering that they can afford a computer. It no longer costs $20,000 or more to buy a small business system. Some businesses actually do quite a bit of work with systems that cost less than $2,000. These small systems won't keep track of ITT's cash flow, but they will do many jobs very nicely.

O.K., so now you're interested. Where do we go from here? A good starting place is a local computer store. A lot of places sell small computers today. Try your local ATARI Home Computer retailer, for example. You will have an opportunity to see ATARI Computers in action. Atari, Inc. has set up an extensive network of computer retailers that range from computer stores to large department stores.

When you visit a computer retailer you may have a communications problem. The salesperson may either know too much or too little and you may think they're speaking in a foreign language. Don't become disheartened by this. We are going to tell you how to do the research on your own. This is exactly what you do when you buy a car or a microwave oven. Buying a computer is no different. There are very few people around who can tell you just what you need to know. It is quite possible to end up with a salesperson who knows less about computers than you do, especially where computers are a small and perhaps unimportant sideline. To an appliance or stereo salesperson, the computer may be just another machine like a dishwasher, dryer, or range (Yes ma'am, would you like one in coppertone or jungle green?).

In all fairness though, the salesperson may be the same kind of informed consumer you want to be. In fact, he or she may even own a computer. You'll just have to learn as much as you can and be prepared.

The retail computer store was one of the most exciting new businesses of the seventies. You will meet real experts there. They may not, however, be able to talk to you on a level you understand. Most computer stores were started by computer hobbyists—another word for fanatic when it comes to computers. Many such hobbyists can't understand why anyone would not want to learn everything there is to know about computers. To the devout, there is no middle ground. If you like computers, you *really* like them. It's hard for the hobbyists to understand that some people just want to use the computer as a tool, not adopt it into the family.

This is not to say that a computer store isn't a good place to buy a computer, because it is. Some of them just take a little effort. The remainder of this book will help you deal with the problems of buying a computer. Be prepared, for instance, to experience some confusion when you go into a computer store. The technical jargon there may be wall-to-wall; terms like RAM and ROM, Pascal and BASIC, DOS and disk may abound. You'll find out what the most important terms mean as you read this book, and we have included a glossary, so hang in there. In fact, we urge beginners to read this book all the way through before making that first serious computer-buying safari (short sorties and patrols are O.K., though).

Throughout this book you will notice a general emphasis on ATARI Home Computer products. We wanted to write a good general introduction to small computers and feel that this can best be done by using one computer as an example all the way through the book. The ATARI Computer is an excellent choice for this for two reasons: friendliness and graphics. Between us we have had experience with most of the small computers available today. We can say without hesitation that, for most applications, the ATARI Computers are the best computer available for the price.

Before we go on, let's talk briefly about the two factors that make the ATARI 400 Computer and the ATARI 800 Computer standouts. *Friendliness,* or *user friendliness,* is a term used to describe ease of operation. We can't overemphasize how important this is to a beginner.

ATARI's documentation is a good example of user friendliness. For instance, here is a quote from the ATARI 400 Computer owner's guide, "This booklet tells you how to install your ATARI 400 Computer in ten easy steps. All you need to do is install the TV Switch Box, connect the computer console to your TV set, plug it into the wall and insert a cartridge. The only tool you'll need is a regular screwdriver." The best part is that the steps are easy and well defined. ATARI Computer programs are the same way; when they tell how to do something, it is in clear, easy-to-understand terms.

If you buy an ATARI Computer, you can take it home, hook it up, plug in a cartridge and it works. If it doesn't, you can call 800-538-8547, from anywhere in the continental United States, and someone will help you (from California, you'll have to call 800-672-1430). The call is free and so is the help. Now that is a friendly thing to do, but Atari, Inc. takes it one step further. You'll get someone who can actually answer a question. We called the Atari number and asked a technical question. The woman who answered was not only pleasant and helpful but she also knew the answer to the question. Other companies provide a toll free number, but in many cases you will have to wait for your answer to come in the mail, if you get it at all.

Another outstanding feature of ATARI Computers is graphics. Graphics is the ability of the computer to display images on the screen. Atari has many years of experience in both arcade games and video games, so they know a lot about graphics. When they do a simulation of a starship, you get the feel of a starship. When they show you how to do a bar chart for a sales presentation, the bar chart is both dramatic and effective. Beyond that though, they have designed a graphics system that can easily be programmed by anyone. People who know absolutely nothing about computers, can be creating their own graphics within a few hours. If you try to do that on another computer you will find out how important friendliness is and how sensational an ATARI Computer really is. We hope we haven't overemphasized friendliness, but it is probably better than telling you that all computers are easy to use, when in reality they are not.

The rest of this book is written and organized so that you can skip around, if you want to. As we introduce each chapter, we will tell which ATARI Computer would be appropriate. There are four ATARI kits that combine all of the accessories you need for a particular application. If a kit is appropriate, we'll describe it.

Chapter 3, HOME, HOME ON THE COMPUTER (WHERE THE RAM AND THE ROM ROAM), starts with an example of how one family uses a computer system. It then discusses the six major areas of home use. In entertainment, games such as STAR RAIDERS™ and MISSILE COMMAND™ are introduced. For this application you will want THE ATARI ENTERTAINER.™ It comes with a pair of Joystick Controllers and two of the world's most exciting computer games. Personal development then shows how a piano student learned syncopation, and it talks about how you can use a computer for self-education. If, after reading this chapter, you want to learn how to write your own programs, you will want to look at THE PROGRAMMER™. It comes with an ATARI BASIC Computing Language cartridge, the *ATARI BASIC Reference Manual* and the *ATARI BASIC Self-Teaching Guide*. The Guide teaches you how to program in easy-to-follow steps. Personal finance and record-keeping show you how a computer can help you balance your checkbook, make investments, stay within your budget, and outwit the taxman. In hobby and recreational computing, you'll see how a computer can help you print a newsletter or keep the stats on your favorite hobby. We finish the chapter with a discussion of home control and health.

Chapters 2, 4, 6, 8, and 10 all deal with the crucial task of selecting the right computer and accessories for your needs and buying them. Chapter 2, HOW TO BUY YOUR OWN COMPUTER outlines seven buying steps that will help you buy the computer that's right for you. We then introduce you to some of the computer features you will want to look at and what is good and bad about those features. The other four chapters show you how to match a computer to a particular need.

One of the most exciting uses of a small computer is communication. In Chapter 5, THE OUTER LIMITS: COMMUNICATING WITH THE WORLD, you will find out how you can tie into someone else's information base; i.e., CompuServe®[1] Information Service, THE SOURCE, AMERICA'S INFORMATION UTILITY®[2] and so on. You will be introduced to new ideas like electronic mail, networks, teleconferencing and information management and you will have access to newswires such as UPI, AP and DOW JONES/NEWS RETRIEVAL®[3] Service. Atari has a nice kit for this application also. It is called THE COMMUNICATOR.™ It consists of a TeleLink™ 1 cartridge, an ATARI 850™ Interface Module, and an ATARI 830™ Acoustic Modem, so you can send and receive information over any standard telephone. You also receive a free hour of connect time to the DOW JONES/NEWS RETRIEVAL Service, the CompuServe Information Service and THE SOURCE, AMERICA'S INFORMATION UTILITY.

If you are interested in education, you will want to read Chapter 7, THE TEACHING MACHINE. Here you will see how the computer can help you learn things yourself or teach your children. If you are a teacher, you will find some ideas for using a computer in your classroom. You will see why THE EDUCATOR,™ another ATARI kit, is a useful classroom tool. It comes with the ATARI 410™ Program Recorder that loads your programs, an ATARI BASIC cartridge, and the

---

[1]Registered trademark of CompuServe, Inc., an H & R Block Company.
[2]THE SOURCE and AMERICA'S INFORMATION UTILITY are service marks of Source Telecomputing Corporation, a subsidiary of The Reader's Digest Association, Inc.
[3]Registered trademark of Dow Jones & Company, Inc.

STATES & CAPITALS program. All you do is insert the ATARI BASIC cartridge, plug in the cassette recorder and put the cassette containing the program into the recorder – the computer takes it from there. There are many education programs available, so we end the chapter with a short survey of programs that aid learning.

Can you use a computer in your business? You'll find the answer to this question in Chapter 9, SOLVING BUSINESS AND PROFESSIONAL PROBLEMS. The chapter starts with a computer application in a small business and then discusses the factors you should consider before computerizing your business. However, you don't have to own your own business to be able to get a lot out of a computer. The last part of the chapter discusses word processing and other managerial applications that are appropriate for anyone.

A computer is nothing more than a box with plastic and wires in it until someone tells it what to do. Chapter 11, THE STUFF THAT MAKES IT HAPPEN: SOFTWARE, will help you understand how to talk to a computer.

You don't have to know anything about automotive mechanics to drive your car and you don't have to know anything about computer electronics to operate a computer. But, if you would like to know a little bit about computer electronics, you will want to read Chapter 12, IT'S NOT MAGIC: THE BASIC COMPUTER™. This chapter presents a brief overview of a typical computer system. You'll find out about terms such as RAM, ROM, serial and parallel and about how the various components of a computer go together to become a working system.

Chapter 13, THE CURRENT CROP, is a survey of currently available small computers. We have included a rating chart that will help you decide which computer is best for you.

There are a lot of things we don't know about computers, but we can tell you where to find out the other things you want to know. In every chapter, we have given you the titles of a few books or magazines that you might want to read. In addition, we have surveyed book and magazine publishers in Chapter 14, WHERE TO FIND EVERYTHING WE DIDN'T TELL YOU. The book ends with a short glossary of the terms you are most likely to encounter.

THE BASIC COMPUTER™

ATARI Home Computer Starter Kits

THE EDUCATOR™

THE COMMUNICATOR™

THE ENTERTAINER™

THE PROGRAMMER™

The home computer is one of the most exciting inventions in all of history. It gives you the opportunity to interact with the world around you in ways that weren't possible five years ago and new applications are being introduced almost daily. We wrote this book for the beginner who wants to know four things: what computers can do today, what in particular a computer can do for you, how to use a computer, and how to select the computer and accessories required for the applications that interest you. When you're finished reading this book, these questions should all be answered and you will be well on your way to something that will be increasingly important in the coming years – computer literacy. If, after reading this book, you decide to buy a computer, drop a line. We'd like to hear how you use it. You can write us in care of dilithium Press, P.O. Box 606, Beaverton, OR 97075.

Chapter 2

How To Buy Your Own Computer

It's hard to concentrate on the tedious job of buying a computer when you're thinking of all the things you can do with a computer. There are galaxies to save, letters to write, books to balance, and things to learn. As you look through the magazines and browse at computer stores you may already be picturing yourself sitting in front of your own computer working (or playing) away on something that interests you. There may be a strong temptation simply to call up a friend who already has a computer and find out what he or she bought. That would be an easy way to buy a computer, but it may not give you the best system for your particular situation.

Buying a computer is hard work. Shopping for a color television or a microwave oven is much simpler since these appliances are both single function devices. Computers, on the other hand, are versatile, multifunction devices, that can do many things – they entertain, teach, keep financial records, and much, much more. Not all personal computers, however, do everything equally well. Therefore, a first step in selecting a computer is to identify the jobs you want it to do.

STEP ONE. IDENTIFY MAJOR USES

It may seem simplistic and obvious to say you need to decide just what you want the computer to do. You would probably be surprised, though, at the number of people who buy a computer with only a vague idea of exactly how they will use it. Suppose you visit a local computer store and take a fancy to a particular computer. It may show well in the store. The programs for it are well written: they execute with little, if any, difficulty, and the results may appear in excellent color with quality graphics. After buying the system you may decide that your primary use will be word processing with games as a secondary use. Unfortunately, you may find that the computer you bought is very good for games and educational uses, but virtually impossible to use as a word processor. In all likelihood, for the same amount of money you could have purchased a system that is great for word processing and good or even fantastic for games and recreational uses.

The first step, then, is the most important. Decide what your major uses will be. Once that's clear, it will be easier to identify the computer systems that are capable of doing the work you want done. Chapters 3, 5, 7, and 9 discuss some of the many potential uses of a computer.

STEP TWO. SOFTWARE CONSIDERATIONS

A computer will not do anything until it has a program (a set of instructions) to follow. Computer programs or *software* can be obtained in two ways. You can write your own programs or you can buy *canned* programs that run on your computer. Many people do a little of both. They may buy most of the programs they regularly use, and write their own programs for specialized applications.

If you plan to write your own programs it will be important to look carefully at the *languages* understood by any computer you are considering. Most personal computers can be programmed in BASIC, a very popular language today. In addition, other languages, such as PILOT, are available for some but not all personal computers. Chapter 11 covers computer languages and software in more detail.

If you don't yet know how to program a computer and want to learn, pay careful attention to the teaching aids available with each computer. Are the manuals clear and easy to understand, can you get teaching aids, such as computer assisted instruction programs, that help you learn the computer language you will use, and do you have a choice of languages?

A variety of software is available for ATARI Home Computers.

Although learning to program a computer can be both interesting and very useful, a large percentage of the people who use personal computers today cannot write their own programs. Instead, they buy programs written by others. Many of us, for example, can't play a note, but that doesn't keep us from buying and enjoying records, albums, and tapes.

If you plan to buy programs for the computer you select, be sure there are programs to buy. There are a few computers which have gained such wide acceptance that many different companies sell all sorts of programs for them. Since, without software, a computer is just a bunch of parts, the variety and quality of software available for a particular computer becomes an important point to consider when buying a system.

With most of the major small computers you will probably be able to buy at least one or two programs in each of the major applications areas. Newer computers, and those from less well accepted manufacturers, have not attracted as much interest from independent programmers, and there is no guarantee that a large number of suitable programs will be available. Unfortunately, the newer machines tend to be the ones with the most sophisticated features. The buyer may thus be caught in a dilemma that pits an older model with lots of software against a new model with many desirable features. Fortunately the manufacturers of new models are beginning to recognize this problem. Atari, for example, is spending a substantial amount of money and corporate energy on developing a large software selection for their computers. Atari has one of the largest in-house program development groups in the industry. In addition, they provide encouragement and support to independent software developers who want to write programs for the ATARI Computers. Through a series of regional centers Atari provides seminars, answers specific questions, and offers assistance to programmers. Through the ATARI Software Acquisition Program, Atari, Inc. reviews and licenses software developed by independent producers. Through another program, the ATARI Program Exchange (APX), Atari, Inc. provides a direct distribution outlet for software written by ATARI Home Computer users, and accepted by APX. In fact, many programs available through APX were written at home by individuals just like you. The APX catalog contains descriptions of all sorts of programs. These programs can be ordered by mail from the the ATARI Program Exchange or purchased at many retailers.

As a result of these efforts, the ATARI Computers, though relatively new, already have a large program base, and the number is continually growing.

STEP THREE. SPECIFY MINIMUM REQUIREMENTS AND PREFERRED KEY FEATURES

Once you clearly specify the major uses, you will need to identify the features a computer must have to do those jobs. For instance, computers used as a word processor must have a keyboard that permits fast touch typing. A typewriter style keyboard is superior to a small calculator style keyboard. This is just the first of a number of minimum requirements for word processing. There must, of course, be a good word processing program available for the computer. It would be nice to have a video display that can put 24 lines of 80 characters on the screen at one time. This is a nice feature, but it is one of those that can greatly increase your cost. You can do very nicely with a display of 24 lines of 40 characters or 16 lines of 62 characters (but not with 22 lines of 23 characters). Several computers with the 24 by 40 or 16 by 62 format are available at an affordable price. The ATARI 800 Computer, which has a 24 by 40 format, has a sohpisticated word processing program for it that uses some unique programs to simulate an 80 (or larger) character line on the screen. See Chapter 9 for more information on the ATARI Word Processor.

None of the requirements noted above for word processing is essential, perhaps not even desirable, in a computer that is to be used solely for entertainment. Instead, you may want to consider characteristics such as whether the computer has a color display, high quality graphics, many recreational programs, and provisions for plugging in game paddles. The final section of this chapter discusses a number of potential characteristics or features for computers. Few people will find all of them equally important. Your intended uses will determine which features are crucial, which are important, and which are of little importance. When you finish this step you should have a list of minimum requirements a computer should have to satisfy your primary needs.

STEP FOUR. IDENTIFY LIKELY SECONDARY USES AND DESIRABLE MACHINE FEATURES

Suppose you've narrowed your choice down to two computers. Both will do your major jobs well, both cost about the same. The choice may come down to the secondary use capabilities. For example, if your family has a strong interest in music, you may want to consider the music generation programs available for the two computers. If one computer has built-in features that allow you to compose and play music it may get the nod over the other one. Even if you don't buy the programs that let you express your musical talents with the computer, it might be a good idea to buy the computer that allows you to add this feature, inexpensively, later.

STEP FIVE. DECIDE HOW MUCH YOU WANT TO SPEND – NOW AND LATER

Now comes the crunch. If your finances are anything like ours, you may have to compromise. It is possible today to buy a complete, fully functional computer with prices that range from $300 to over $2 million. Personal computer prices begin at about the same price as a color TV.

In the last three years, we've been involved in buying over 30 different computer systems. In every case, had we been able to spend $500 to $1000 more, we would have selected a different computer. With some exceptions, you get useful features for the money you pay when it comes to buying a computer. The trick is to spend the money on the features you need. Don't spend money for something you don't need, and don't waste money buying a computer that doesn't have the features required for your application.

Another price consideration to keep in mind is how much you may have to spend later. We know of an owner who purchased a system for a very good price only to discover that the cost of expanding that system was very high. If, at some time in the future, you plan to buy additional equipment for your computer, be sure the cost will be reasonable.

Finally, a potential shock for the new owner is the cost of service. Some companies, such as Atari, maintain regional repair centers that provide good service at a fair price. Atari has a strong dealer training program as well.

A few manufacturers have little or no service in much of the U.S. The owner of one such *orphan* system was told that even minor service would cost $120 plus parts each time a serviceperson looked at the equipment. This may be typical and expected in the business world where large, complicated systems must be kept at peak operating efficiency, but small computer owners are likely to find the cost excessive. Be sure that the computer you select has good service and an excellent warranty.

STEP SIX. TRY THEM OUT

Now that you know how you want to use a computer and have a fairly good idea of what is affordable, you can begin the tire-kicking phase. Chapter 13 contains descriptions of the major small computers available at the end of 1981. It is only a starting place, however, since new and improved models are being introduced on a fairly regular basis. More up-to-date information can be obtained by visiting local computer stores, or department stores that handle personal computers, and from reading current issues of magazines such as *Interface Age, Microcomputer, Creative Computing, Compute, Infoworld, Personal Computing,* and *Popular Computing.*

We would suggest you limit yourself to computers already on the market rather than those announced as being available *in the near future.* In this industry the near future can be as long as three years. In some cases, new models which are announced (and for which orders are accepted) never appear.

The same sort of problem can happen with computer accessories. If you want a computer with a compatible printer from the same company, for example, look only at systems with acceptable printers already available and working rather than systems for which a fantastic printer is *in the works.*

One final point. No amount of reading reviews will take the place of a hands-on demonstration. The computer you finally select should be one you have tried out personally – one you know is easy and comfortable for you to use. Be sure and try it before you buy it.

STEP SEVEN. SURVEY SOURCES

Steps 6 and 7 should probably be completed at the same time. As you check out computers for suitability, also evaluate the potential sources of supply. Most computers are purchased from one of three sources: a local retail store, a mail order supplier, or the manufacturer. Fewer and fewer manufacturers are willing to sell directly to consumers. Most prefer instead to deal with distributors and dealers who, in turn, sell to consumers. This frees the factory to concentrate on production and development. They then count on their dealers or separate service centers to provide most of the customer service.

The other two alternatives, retail stores and mail order suppliers, are a mixed bag. There are excellent examples of ethical, responsible businesses in both categories. There are also examples of plain crooks, inept ne'er-do-wells, and fast buck olympians in both categories. If you are considering buying a computer that is supposed to be serviced by the retailer, a good local store with a top-notch technician who provides timely service is a valuable commodity. Prices at such a store may be a bit higher than they are from mail order discounters, but most people feel the slightly higher price is worth it to have the person responsible for the warranty just down the street. If you're not sure about a store, take the time to get opinions from computer owners in your area. We once considered buying a computer from a local dealer so we could get quick service. You can imagine how we felt when we discovered the dealer had no service personnel at all for that computer. When a system went down (needed repair) it was shipped back to the factory in California. Since the dealer's price was $200 more than the mail order price, we reconsidered the purchase. Apparently many other people did the same. The store is no longer in business.

Few generalizations can be made about mail order computer companies. Some have good track records. Many mail order suppliers have a staff of service technicians and provide timely repair service. Others are slow at delivering goods in the first place and even slower at handling service requests. One way to protect yourself is to read the letters and commentaries about mail order companies in the computer magazines and talk with other computer owners in your area who purchase equipment by mail. In general, you will avoid most of these problems if you buy from a retailer.

STEP EIGHT. BUY IT.

There's not much else to do. Once you've done your home-work go out and buy yourself a computer.

POTENTIALLY IMPORTANT FEATURES

Video Displays

All the popular home computer models use a video display for normal operation of the computer. All video displays are not created equal, however. Some computers display as few as 12 lines on the screen at one time and have 32 or fewer characters on each line. That is a little on the skimpy side. The standard displays for small computers can put either 24 lines of 40 characters or 16 lines of 62 characters on the screen at once. More expensive systems use a 24 by 80 format. The display can be either a monitor attached to the computer or a television or monitor that is separate from the computer. The separate monitor or television has at least two advantages over the attached monitor. First, it can be used elsewhere when you are not using it with the computer. Next, it gives you a lot of flexibility in arranging your key-board. (We southpaws love this feature, and you will too.)

For home computing, educational applications, and some business applications two other features, color and graphics, are more important than the character display capacity. Several models now offer color displays rather than the tradi-tional black and white. Color adds zest to games and makes computer-aided learning more interesting.

Most computers also have at least some graphics capability. That means, in addition to letters and numbers, the computer can display figures, graphs, charts, game boards, or compu-ter-generated pictures on the screen. On some computers the graphics features are limited but useful. Other computers, on the other hand, can handle very sophisticated graphics. In ad-dition to educational and game applications, businesses can use color graphics to create sales displays as well as charts and figures.

As we mentioned before, the ATARI 800 and 400 Compu-ters both have exceptional color graphics. The ATARI Com-puters allow you to write your own BASIC programs us-ing the same high quality graphics the company program-

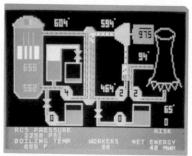

SCRAM™ (A NUCLEAR
POWER PLANT SIMULATION)

MISSILE COMMAND™

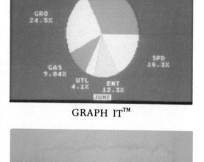

GRAPH IT™

*The ATARI Computers have
exceptional color graphics.*

STOCK CHARTING*

mers use to create game cartridges. On some other computers
you can watch it create beautiful pictures on the screen, but
the machine is built in a way that keeps owners from writing
programs that achieve the same level of quality.

Two other points should be made about video display.
First, while most computers have video display *capacity,*
many do not come with video monitors. Some are designed to
be connected to a standard television, and some require you
to buy a video monitor. Monitors cost from $125 to $700
depending on their quality and whether the monitor is color
or black and white. Second, while all systems will display let-

*A Control Data CYBERWARE™ product manufactured under
license from Control Data Corporation ©1980.

ters and numbers, some display only upper case or capital letters. We prefer a display with both upper and lowercase letters, but your pattern of usage will determine whether that feature is important.

Keyboard

Perhaps we're fanatics about keyboards, but they can determine whether working with the computer is a joy or a pain. Some manufacturers are producing computers with midget-sized keyboards resembling those on calculators. The keys are small and closely spaced, and if you have large fingers, like we do, they are hard to use without making errors. There is simply no way to touch type on these tiny keyboards. In 1980, we bought a computer after reading several ads about it in the electronics magazines. It was an interesting machine with many features for an unheard of price ($150). Unfortunately, it uses a tiny *touch sensitive* keyboard that requires you to press firmly on a flat sheet of plastic to key anything into the computer. The task proved so difficult that we rarely use the computer.

The sight of a full-sized typewriter-style keyboard on your intended computer, however, does not mean all is well. A good keyboard should offer smooth resistance to the touch without catching, and the whole assembly should be firmly mounted with no flexing or *give* in the keyboard when you press a key. Finally, the keyboard should be free of *keybounce*. You have keybounce when you type an A on the keyboard and AA or AAA appears on the screen. Keyboards with contact points exposed to dust are particularly susceptible to keybounce. Atari has taken steps to avoid keybounce in their machines. We have not experienced keybounce on an ATARI Computer.

The ATARI 800 Home Computer uses a very good standard size keyboard while the ATARI 400 Home Computer uses a touch sensitive, *membrane* keyboard. (A membrane keyboard is one solid piece of material.) The keyboard on the ATARI 400 Computer is functional and less expensive than a typewriter style keyboard. The membrane keyboards are fine for games and for running canned programs. Since membrane keyboards are impervious to spills and are also dustproof they are the preferred type if you plan to use the computer in some environments (e.g. in a dusty warehouse, in an elementary school, or with young children who like to use the computer while drinking their milk).

Membrane keyboards are not very good for word processing or for projects that require you to spend many hours writing programs for the computer. Before selecting a computer, sit down at the keyboard and work with it for a while. Consider your probable uses for the system and decide whether the keyboard will be acceptable to you.

Power Supply

Most of the power supplies in current models are at least adequate. The virtues and vices of power supplies are discussed in more detail in Chapter 12.

Storage Medium Options

Virtually all personal computers have compatible cassette storage systems. Programs or data you want to save and use again later can be recorded on regular (but good quality) audio cassettes. Cassette storage is cheap, generally reliable, and easy to use. Unfortunately, it is slow. A large program can take three minutes or more to load. That may not sound like a long time now, but when you're sitting in front of the computer it can seem like forever, particularly if there are problems with the load and you have to do it again...and again...and again. (It is also easy to end up with a hundred or more tapes.) Finding the one you need can take longer than a visit to the dentist. Actually, we should not be so negative about cassette storage. Good systems can be very pleasant and easy to use. A poorly designed one, however, is very trying. Our experience with the ATARI 410™ Program Recorder has been extremely positive. It loads programs into the computer reliably. In addition, the cassette circuits of ATARI Computers were designed with the user in mind. The computer provides signals (tones) that tell you when to press the play or record buttons, and as the computer reads the data on the cassette, it provides a sound through the television speaker that lets you know everything is proceeding properly.

A popular alternative to cassette storage is the *floppy diskette*. Users with a floppy disk system use small diskettes that look like 45 RPM records as a program or data storage medium rather than cassette tapes. When used, a diskette slides into a slot in a disk drive. The disk drive then spins the diskette and reads or writes information on the diskette.

Disk drives are fast, very reliable, and as you might expect, more expensive than cassette recorders. Count on paying at least $500, perhaps as much as $900, for a small single drive system. Dual drive systems cost even more. For the money, you get a high speed, reliable storage system that can put many programs on each of the little 5¼-inch disks. Many computers for businesses have built-in disk drives in lieu of cassette systems. They are generally in the $3000+ price range, but give businesses the speed and storage capacity required for large scale applications. Disk drives can also be added to most personal computers as well.

Actually, disk drives come in two sizes (5¼ inches and 8 inches). The capacity of the diskettes vary according to size and type, but a great deal of data can be stored with even the smallest, least sophisticated disk drive. While there have been some quality control problems with a few of the disk drive manufacturers, many of these have been corrected. The overall level of quality in disk drives is reasonably high.

Base Cost and Expansion Costs

It is probably natural to compare computer prices by looking at the price tag on the computer. But that may not tell all the story. Consider a familiar example. When you shop for a new car, the sticker prices on two cars can vary by as much as $5000 even when both cars are on the same dealer lot and are the same make and model. The difference in sticker price can be accounted for by options. One may have air conditioning, power steering and brakes, a moon roof, special accent and protective molding, a special engine and transmission, special paint job, and an optional AM/FM stereo cassette player. The same thing can happen with computers. One dealer may quote you a very low price for a computer while another dealer may offer to sell you a system for hundreds of dollars more. The higher bid may mean the dealer has listened to you describe what you would like to do with your computer and is offering a system that includes all the accessories you will need to do that job. There is the *base* price of the computer, and there is the cost of *expanding* the computer to do a particular job. The base price may not include the cost of a cassette recorder, disk drive, extra memory, or a printer. Many first time buyers of computers are shocked to find that the cost of accessories can easily add up to several times the cost of the computer itself. We are used to buying a $7000 car and looking at options and accessories that cost only a fraction of the cost of the car. With a computer, it is possible to buy disk drives or printers that cost much more than the computer. That means the base price of the computer is really not that important to many people. The important number is the cost of expanding the system to do the work you want it to do. It would be easy for a company to put a very competitive price on their computer to attract buyers and then to make the cost of expanding the system very high. This has been done by several companies.

The point is, always consider the cost of expanding a basic system to meet your specific needs, not just the price of a *bare bones* computer. A positive point for ATARI Computers is their modularity. Even if you plan eventually to have a system that includes many accessories, it is not necessary to buy everything at once. You can buy a basic ATARI Computer, use it for many different applications immediately, and add additional components later as your interests and needs change and grow.

Chapter 3

Home, Home on the Computer
(Where the RAM and the ROM Roam)

Not long ago a student in one of Jerry's courses on educational computing mentioned that she and her husband had taken the plunge. They had ordered their own computer! Thinking everyone was in the same state of inflationary poverty that has a long-term lease on our bank accounts, we assumed the happy owners had scraped together enough to buy a simple, under $500, computer. Actually, the cost of their system was well over $2,000. They had purchased a popular computer with extra memory, a printer, a monitor, two disk drives, and several hundred dollars worth of programs.

When you can buy a very good computer for the home for the cost of a color television why would a middle-class family spend $2000 on a computer system? This family had several reasons. They enjoy games and feel that the variety of recreational programs available for their computer will keep them entertained for years. The computer also serves as a home tutor for their children. Also, as a high school teacher, the mother wanted a computer that would help her keep track of grades in the classes she teaches. Both she and her husband are looking forward to learning BASIC and have several ideas they hope to turn into working programs.

Is this the typical *computer family?* Not really. In fact, there is no such thing as typical when it comes to computer owners. Most potential buyers want to use their computer for one or two major applications. Those *major* applications are the ones you use to justify buying the system in the first place. A friend of ours, for example, is a research psychologist at a center for retarded adults and writes a number of articles and monographs each year. He bought his computer for statistical analysis and word processing. (Word processing is the term used to describe the use of computers to write and edit documents electronically. Word processing is described in more detail in Chapter 9).

For most people, there will also be some, perhaps many, secondary reasons for buying a computer. These secondary reasons by themselves aren't enough to justify buying a computer, but once it is bought, the secondary uses can actually take up more of the computer's time than the major uses.

We are frequently asked the question *What can I do with a computer?* It is a simple question, but one that is very difficult to answer for a particular person or family. The computer is much like an artist's blank canvas or a sculptor's block of stone. The outcome will depend on the artist or the user. In this chapter we will try to give you an idea of what you can do with your computer.

ENTERTAINMENT

Many people say they are buying their computer for another reason, but the A-number-one use of computers in the home is fun. That is not to say the computers aren't used to do other things like balancing your checkbook. They are. But you only balance your checkbook when you have to. It's not something you look forward to after a long day at the office. Playing games, composing music, or drawing color *pictures* on the screen are a lot more fun. The checks can wait until tomorrow night.

Under the category ENTERTAINMENT we have selected several programs for ATARI® Home Computers that serve as examples of the type of material available.

When we told one friend we were writing a computer book that focused on ATARI Home Computers, he began to enthusiastically describe an ATARI game that kept him glued to his keyboard for hours. With a Ph.D. in electrical engineering and years of computer experience, he is not one to be easily impressed by a new computer game. The game that caught his attention is STAR RAIDERS™. The concept behind it is not new. Games with the same premise have been out for many years. You are the pilot of a star fighter in space and a group of alien ships has entered your galaxy intent on destroying your space stations (and you). The plot may not be new, but the way the game is played is. The ATARI STAR RAIDERS game is the most realistic simulation of flying through space we have ever seen. Stars whiz by, enemy ships close in and fire their photon torpedos at you. As you fire back (by pressing a button on the Joystick Controller), the torpedos leave a trail as they head toward their target. A hit produces a colorful explosion on the screen along with realistic sound effects. You have at your disposal a command computer that displays important information at the bottom of the screen (fuel supply, location of enemy ships, damage reports). The computer will also help you aim at enemy ships in an interstellar dogfight if you wish.

STAR RAIDERS can be played at several levels from Novice to Commander. We do fairly well at the Novice level but have never been able to survive much past 4 minutes at the Commander level. On occasion, Starfleet command has reduced our rank to *Galactic Cook* or *Garbage Scow Captain* after a particularly poor performance. Atari has years of experience in the video arcade field and their computer, as well as their game, shows it. Atari also markets a game called SPACE INVADERS* which requires players to fire moon based laser cannons at hundreds of invaders who are trying to land on the moon. If you drop by virtually any video arcade you can watch confirmed SPACE INVADERS freaks drop quarter after quarter in the arcade version of this game.

---

*SPACE INVADERS is a trademark of Taito America Corporation

Other games available for ATARI Computers include SUPER BREAKOUT,™ a sort of electronic tennis or handball which can be played by one to eight players. Again, the color graphics, sound, and specially designed paddle controllers make this version particularly good.

Simulations of competitive team sports like football, baseball, and basketball are also popular computer games as are blackjack, checkers, chess, and Tic-Tac-Toe. Atari has a 3D version of Tic-Tac-Toe which turns that relatively simple game into a challenging one. You can play against someone else or the computer. Play against the computer is also possible with the COMPUTER CHESS program from Atari. The computer displays a chessboard in color and then plays against you at any of eight levels of difficulty. Chess pieces are moved by tilting the Joystick Controller in the direction you want a piece to move. At the higher levels of difficulty the computer can be hard to beat.

Games such as STAR RAIDERS™, BASKETBALL, COMPUTER CHESS, SUPER BREAKOUT, SPACE INVADERS and 3–D TIC-TAC-TOE are packaged in cartridges. To play the game it is only necessary to insert the cartridge in a slot on top of the computer. Games like BLACKJACK come on cassettes. You place them in the ATARI 410 Program Recorder and instruct the computer to load the programs into the computer's memory before play begins.

The popularity of ATARI Home Computers means there are enough owners to make it profitable for vendors other than Atari to market games (as well as other types of programs). The computer magazine *Compute!* (P.O. Box 5406, Greensboro, North Carolina 27403) has a section of the magazine devoted to ATARI Computers. Current issues carry ads for many games including backgammon and a computer version of Tank Trap. *Creative Computing* (P.O. Box 789-M, Morristown, New Jersey 07906, 800-631-8112) and *Micro* (Box 6502, Chelsmford, MA 01824) also have columns on ATARI Computers and quite a few ads for programs.

PERSONAL DEVELOPMENT

The computer can be a very effective learning tool. We have devoted an entire chapter to educational computing, but it seems appropriate to present a few examples of programs

STAR RAIDERS™ is exciting and challenging. ⟶

that promote individual growth and learning in this section as well. The programs described below are all designed to be used in the home. Chapter 7 describes many more educational applications, some of which are also appropriate for home use (e.g. a touch typing course and foreign language programs). Other programs are more likely to be used in schools.

For families with musical interests there is an ATARI cartridge called MUSIC COMPOSER™. Several computers can produce at least simple sounds. A few can be programmed to generate complex musical tones. The ATARI Computer can create tones that have up to four *voices,* a feature that would cost thousands of dollars just a few years ago. With the MUSIC COMPOSER program, your ATARI Computer can be used to actually compose music. As you type in notes on the keyboard, a musical staff appears on the screen. You can then edit or modify your composition, save it on disk or tape, and listen as the computer plays your music through the television speaker or a stereo with an appropriate input jack. It is a sophisticated program that is both entertaining and educational. A review of the MUSIC COMPOSER by Karl and David Zinn appeared in *Creative Computing* (April, 1981). The Zinns, experienced computer users, described several applications of the program at home and at school. Some music for piano was input and played to help a piano student understand some points about syncopation that were unclear to him. In another application, a cornet player in a band programmed band music so she could practice at home with a *band* accompanying her. The accompaniment slowed down or speeded up as needed for practice. In their conclusion the Zinns commented, "Clearly some people thought carefully about what should go into the Music Composer to make it helpful in music education. We hope others who find themselves in the position of advising computer companies will also help make the entertainment products better for education."

Another personal learning product for ATARI Computers is a series of cassettes called AN INVITATION TO PROGRAMMING™. While many computer owners will use *store bought* programs, others may be interested in writing their own from scratch. AN INVITATION TO PROGRAMMING is an educational program that uses the computer to teach you about computer programming.

PERSONAL FINANCE AND RECORD KEEPING

Well, we've finally come to the work. With a computer, however, it should be easier to balance the checkbook, keep track of investments, or put your coin collection in order. There are programs to help computer owners do virtually all of their financial record keeping. Below are short descriptions of a few illustrative applications:

Budget and Checkbook Balancing

A personal budgeting program helps a family keep track of spending and earning patterns. The more involved programs can even provide an overview of spending and earning trends. Monthly and yearly printouts on spending categories and predicted patterns can be generated. Each month, when checks are written to pay bills, the computer program can speed up the process by providing a display of recurring payments (e.g. mortgage, car payment) as well as incidental bills (e.g. car repairs, oil credit card bills which vary from month to month). The computer can help keep track of bills received, payments made, and information such as the time between receipt and payment, the minimum payment due, the total owed on each account, and the interest paid on each account.

Less ambitious programs just help the family bill payer balance the checkbook when the monthly statement arrives from the bank. The typical checkbook balancing program uses a visual display to organize deposits and disbursements, and asks the user to type in the amount of each check written or deposit made. It then checks your input against the bank statement and identifies any discrepancies. This can save an hour or two each month and helps spot any mistakes you or the bank made.

Investment and Tax Programs

A financial record keeping program leads naturally to the question of whether computers can do anything to uncomplicate that annual American ritual of offering financial sacrifices to the IRS god. Yes, it can. The computer can, for example, help keep track of tax deductible payments and purchases made during a year and provide you with an itemized list with totals at tax time. This one application has saved some owners the cost of the computer. Several companies also sell income tax programs that actually compute your tax each year and fill out the 1040 forms.

The BOOKKEEPER* helps you manage your books.

The computer can also be used to help you make good investment decisions. Atari has four programs in their INVESTMENT ANALYSIS SERIES. One, STOCK ANALYSIS*, can be used to manage a portfolio of stocks. It will calculate the rate of return for each stock on an annual and long term basis, and evaluate a stock in terms of the projected dividend payments it is likely to yield in the future. The program doesn't tell you whether to sell a stock or keep it, but it does provide you with several important pieces of information which can be used in making the decision.

Another program, STOCK CHARTING*, is used to keep track of a stock's performance across days, months, and

---

*A Control Data CYBERWARE™ product manufactured under license from Control Data Corp©1980

The conversational language programs are excellent for self-study or as aids to formal study. ⟶

years. It generates several commonly used values that indicate how a stock is performing (i.e. price variations, number of shares being traded, high and low prices). STOCK CHARTING* can be used to follow several stocks at once with performance data displayed in charts and tables. A third ATARI program, BOND ANALYSIS*, does a similar job for investors interested in the bond market.

If you're like us, you are more likely to be borrowing money than investing it these days. Another ATARI program, MORTGAGE & LOAN ANALYSIS*, can be very useful if you are considering major purchases that must be financed. Recently, when Jerry bought a piece of real estate, his trusty mortgage interest rate books could not be used because they only went up to 12%, a figure that seemed almost criminal only a few years ago. Now it would be much sought after if only it were available. We used MORTGAGE & LOAN ANALYSIS to determine the monthly payments on mortgages at various interest rates (13¾% to 16½%) and on mortgages of varying lengths (20 to 30 years). The program will display information in charts on the screen or print a permanent copy if you have a printer. After considering the likely rate of inflation over the term of the loan, the tax relief provided by interest payments, and the options provided by accepting a favorable second mortgage from the seller, he was able to make an offer that was both financially manageable and economically sound. Using the program considerably reduced the amount of tedious figuring required to compare the various alternatives.

We have really only touched on the more obvious financial applications in this section. There are programs that help you make a decision on whether to buy a particular piece of rental property, programs that manage and keep track of real estate investments, programs that keep track of family property and many, many more. There will be an even wider variety of programs in the future. If financial applications are a particular interest of yours, you may want to read Chapter 9 on business applications and Chapter 5 on communications since several other financial programs are discussed there.

---

*A Control Data CYBERWARE™ product manufactured under license from Control Data Corp© 1980

HOBBY AND RECREATIONAL PROGRAMS

In addition to the games already discussed under ENTER-
TAINMENT, many use their computer in their hobby. An
Oklahoma friend of ours, Jerry Scott, is an ATARI Computer
retailer and a motorcycle rider. Now he isn't one of those
fellows who rides across the country on a big *hog* wearing a
war surplus leather jacket and smelly blue jeans held up by a
length of motorcycle chain. Like Jerry, many members of his
group are community oriented people who own small
businesses. Others are lawyers, engineers, technicians, and
teachers. The Oklahoma group sponsors a type of competitive race called an *enduro*. It is aptly named because it involves trying to endure riding over 100 miles through
swamps, over hills, into rivers, and under fences while maintaining a specified course speed. As in a car rally, riders start
at different times and must arrive at specified *check points*
along the way. A good *enduro* requires a large amount of
record keeping which must be done with to-the-second preci-
sion. Accurate and timely scoring is particularly important
for this race, since it is sanctioned by the American Motorcycle Association and points earned by riders count toward
the national championship. Our Oklahoma friend wrote an
enduro scoring program for his computer that not only helps
ensure accuracy, it scores the race and prints out the winners
quicker than was ever possible before.

You may not be interested in using a computer to score
motorcycle races, but it is very likely that a computer can be
used in some aspect of your favorite hobby. Chapter 5 tells
you how to use the computer to check airline schedules and
make vacation or business reservations for flights, car rent-
als, and hotel rooms. If you have an extensive collection of
stamps, coins, or whatever, you can use a computer to keep a
categorized and catalogued inventory of your collection.

If you belong to a club, religious group, or organization
with many members you can use a computer's word processing talents to write and print a newsletter. Then you can use a
mailing list program to keep track of members' addresses and
to print mailing labels for each issue. The MAILING LIST
program for ATARI Computers can be used to print mailing
labels, keep a Christmas card list, keep track of the addresses
and phone numbers of family and friends, and for many

other purposes. It can even be used to organize information that has nothing to do with addresses. A family with a large collection of tools in many different locations (e.g. basement workshop, garage, summer cottage, office) can use the program to keep an inventory of tools along with their location. The program has features that permit you to get a listing (on the screen or on a printer) of selected categories (e.g. all the tools at the summer cottage, all relatives living in Tennessee, club members with specific interests, etc.) It is a very versatile program that is easy to learn to use.

We could write an entire book on hobby applications of computers, but the examples above should give you an idea of the range of possibilities. Current issues of many computer magazines such as *Popular Computing, Creative Computing, Interface Age,* and *Personal Computing* will usually have articles about other uses in this category.

HOME CONTROL

We have included this category of application because it is frequently discussed in popular magazines and in newspaper articles about computing. A typical article will describe how a computer can be programmed to keep the house at a certain temperature, how it can turn on the coffee pot a few minutes before you get up in the morning, and so on. A computer can, indeed, be programmed to control the environment in your home. It will keep the temperature just right, water the begonias when their soil is dry, and circulate air through the solar collectors when the sun is shining and the house is cold. The problem with this scenario, however, is one of overkill. The coffee pot can be turned on by a $4.95 timer just as well as by a $500 computer. In fact, all the computer applications which fall under the general category of *home control* will probably be performed, not by a general purpose computer, but by a *dedicated* computer. Many microwave ovens, for example, have computers in them to control the operation of the oven. That computer is dedicated to one job, controlling the oven, and probably costs the oven manufacturer $5 to $15. Some *smart* thermostats also have dedicated computers in them. Dedicated computers are less expensive, and their operation does not tie up a general purpose computer. Using an ATARI 400 Computer, for example, as an intelligent burglar alarm, is certainly possible, but the computer could not be used for anything else while it is watching for burglars. We, therefore, do not expect to see general purpose computers widely used in home control applications in spite of newspaper articles and the appearance of a few model *homes of the future* that use them for that purpose.

COMPUTERS AND HEALTH

This last category of home applications has been given very little attention thus far, but it is one we believe will increase in the future.

The health problems of many individuals require them to follow precisely defined regimens of diet, exercise, or medicine. A computer, for example, has been used to keep track of a diabetic child's blood and urine glucose levels. The computer can also plot trends that indicate whether current insulin dosage levels are appropriate and warn the parents if it appears a pattern is headed toward a problem. Exercise programs, diets, and other types of health related projects can all be improved by using a computer to keep track of progress.

SUMMARY

This concludes our brief summary of home applications. In reality, however, we have described just a few of the things a computer can do in the home. The chapters on business applications, educational applications, and telecommunications all cover ways the computer in your home can be put to use.

We suggest you read the other applications chapters and then visit a retailer that handles ATARI Home Computers. Sit down at the computer and try out some of the programs available for the system. By trying it out yourself you'll get an even better idea of the things you will want to do with your own computer.

Chapter 4

Shopping For A Computer For Your Home

So you've decided to buy a home computer. It will be an exciting day when you bring it home. It is one purchase that every member of the family can use and enjoy. One family member may set aside an hour each day to start studying French or Spanish using a computer assisted instruction program. The kids (and parents too) are likely to spend time playing one of their favorite games such as STAR RAIDERS or SCRAM™ (A Nuclear Power Plant Simulation). You can also use the computer to organize and keep family finances. A high school or college student with a term paper due tomorrow may use the computer's telecommunications features to get access to a government report or Associated Press news release on the topic of the paper and then use the word processing program to write the paper. There are so many things a computer can do.

Now, let's turn our attention to how you can make sure you buy the right home computer for your needs. This short chapter is organized much like Chapter 2 with special attention paid to issues particularly relevant to buying a computer for the home. We'll start with uses.

STEP ONE. IDENTIFY MAJOR USES

This is a difficult step when selecting a home computer. A business computer, for example, may be used for only one or two uses (e.g. word processing and accounting), but a home computer is likely to be used for many things. Saturday night, it may play chess with a budding master; Sunday it may print out mailing labels for a club newsletter; Sunday night it may be the focus of the younger kids as they receive some help with basic math skills.

The home computer has such diverse applications that we recommend you read the chapters on business, educational, and telecommunications uses before making a comprehensive list of intended applications for your home computer.

The educational programs can be enjoyed by the whole family.

STEP TWO. SOFTWARE CONSIDERATIONS

At this point you may be thinking, "I'll never learn to program a computer, so the only thing I need to be concerned with is whether I can buy lots of good canned programs for the computer." We agree, you can get your money's worth from a computer just by using it as an appliance. That is, just load in the program you want to run and use the computer as you would any other appliance in the home.

We feel there are several good reasons to consider learning to program the computer as well. First, it isn't difficult. Computers such as the ATARI 400 and ATARI 800 Home Computers have been designed specifically for first time users. There are many learning aids as well as easy to understand instructions on running the computer and learning to program it in simple languages such as PILOT or BASIC. One of the best aids available is the ATARI kit, THE PROGRAMMER.

In earlier times, reading and writing were special skills learned only by a few people. Each community or settlement, for example, might have a scribe who, for a small fee, would write your letter for you or read a document. During the settlement of the West, some saloons had someone who could write a letter home for a homesick cowboy or a lonely miner. In those days, you could get along nicely without knowing how to read.

Today it is very difficult, if not impossible, to be self-sufficient if you can't read. Illiteracy is a significant handicap in America today. Tomorrow, lack of computer literacy may be a significant limitation. Virtually every profession, every trade, even the way we go about our everyday lives, is being changed and influenced by computers. Having a home computer can give both you and your children a head start on computer literacy – an optional skill today that may not be so optional tomorrow.

The ATARI 400 Computer with the ATARI 410™ Program Recorder and the ATARI 822™ Thermal Printer may meet all your needs.

STEP THREE. SPECIFY MINIMUM REQUIREMENTS AND PREFERRED KEY FEATURES

Video Display

For a home computer we strongly recommend you consider a system that has strong color and graphics features. So many of the home applications are enhanced by color and by the ability to put charts, figures, game boards, and "pictures" on the screen, that you are limiting yourself if you select a computer with a black and white display and limited graphics features. We also recommend that you buy a computer that has special characters. For instance, suppose you want your computer to print out the phrase "I love you", followed by a dozen hearts. It is almost impossible to draw a heart on many computers. An ATARI 400 Home Computer, for instance, uses a heart as a special character.

As long as you are getting color graphics, get sound also. Games, educational programs and many other home applications are greatly enhanced by sound.

The decision to use a color television or a color monitor is a decision that will depend on individual factors. If you already have a color television that is not in constant use you can save some money if you use it. Even if you buy a TV specifically for the computer there may be advantages to buying a TV rather than a monitor since it can be used as a receiver as well as a computer display. A color monitor is often more expensive than a color TV, but it will probably provide a slightly sharper display. The increased crispness may be worth the extra cost, particularly if you also own a videotape or video disk system that can use the monitor as well.

Keyboard

There are two major types of keyboards on computers today—membrane and standard typewriter-style keyboards. Membrane keyboards are less expensive and more resistant to damage from spills and jelly sandwiches. Membrane keyboards are also easier to clean. Standard typewriter–style keyboards, on the other hand, are easier to use. You can touch type on them without difficulty. The type you choose will depend on your particular preferences.

Storage Medium Options

We would estimate that around 70% of the computers purchased for home use are purchased with a cassette tape recorder. We would also estimate that half of these people buy a disk drive within two years.

The ATARI Home Computers have a cassette system that is dependable and reliable. The ATARI 410 Program Recorder is a special unit that has two tracks—one for data and one for audio. The audio track is used in many of the educational programs available from Atari, Inc., and from other vendors. It allows you to hear directions or instructions while viewing something on the screen. For that reason, we recommend you buy the program recorder even if you plan to use a disk drive for data and program storage.

The disk drive is fast and convenient. The extra cost can be justified on that basis alone by many people. If you will be storing and manipulating large amounts of data you may find the disk drive essential. If someone in your family, for example, plans to use the computer to write papers, reports, articles, or books, a disk drive may be required. If you will be using the computer to keep track of the performance of a large number of stocks in an investment portfolio, you will want a disk drive.

User Friendly

An absolute necessity for a home computer is that it be a friendly machine. If the instructions and learning aids that come with the computer are not understandable; if the computer itself was not designed with the user in mind, the machine may gather dust in a corner.

Base Cost and Expansion Costs

Be sure to include the costs of any required accessories. If, for example, you intend to do word processing on the home computer remember to take into consideration the price of a good printer such as the ATARI 825™ 80 Column Printer.

STEP FOUR. IDENTIFY LIKELY SECONDARY USES AND DESIRABLE MACHINE FEATURES

Now we're getting down to business. At this point you should have a relatively clear idea of what you're looking for in a computer. Get them in mind, make a list of the things you must have, the things you would like to have, and the likely secondary uses. Now comes the final pre-shopping consideration, cost.

STEP FIVE. DECIDE HOW MUCH YOU WANT TO SPEND – NOW AND LATER

For most families, the purchase of a computer requires serious thought. Many families can justify the purchase because a computer has so many uses. You may decide to just

Do you need disk storage, cassette storage or both?

buy the computer console first, and then buy the accessories later.

In today's computer market, first time buyers are also often concerned about the timing of their purchase. In our seminars, people always want to know if there is a break-through just over the horizon that will bring the price down and the features up. The answer is both complicated and difficult. It is true that this field changes rapidly. If you wait a

year, the price may be cheaper. Then again, it may not. We don't see any new technology that will make the computer you buy today a horse and buggy that will be passed by a horseless carriage tomorrow.

If we look at another technological development, as an example, we see that the television's history has been one of gradual rather than revolutionary improvement. Many people waited years before buying a television because they expected the price to come down drastically. During some periods the price did drop some, but the people who waited missed a lot of television while they were waiting. Our advice is to buy today, but buy a computer that can be expanded and upgraded as new developments occur. The ATARI Home Computers, for example, are modularized systems. The ATARI 800 Computer has slots for adding extra memory boards, and slots for plugging in new programs. If a new computer language is offered for it, you have a slot on the computer where new language cartridges can be inserted. The modularized design also makes it easier to add new peripherals as they become available.

STEP SIX. TRY THEM OUT.

Now you're prepared to do some serious shopping. Atari has a toll free number ((800) 538-8547 or (800) 672-1430 (within California)) you can call to get the names of local ATARI Home Computer retailers. Visit several stores that sell home computers and have programs demonstrated.

STEP SEVEN. BUY IT.

That's it. Buy it and take it home.

Chapter 5

The Outer Limits: Communicating With the World

Thus far we have discussed applications that are relatively familiar. Using a computer for recreational applications, for learning, and for financial record keeping really isn't all that startling. New technology is just making it easier (or more fun) to do something we've been doing all along. In this chapter, however, it is a bit different. The computer as a communications device is probably the least understood application today; yet it may be the use that puts a computer in virtually every home in the nation. It may, in fact, have an impact on our way of life that parallels the impact of television or the telephone.

Societies have always been concerned with information and with communication. Not only do we want to know, we want to know quickly. The original long distance olympic runners, for example, were honored for their speed partially because they could carry messages quickly. Radios, televisions, telephones, transatlantic cables, communications satellites, and the telegraph are familiar examples of technology that helped us to communicate better and faster.

We are now entering a new era of communication that some feel will change not only the way we get and use information, but the ways we communicate with each other as well. That new era, in fact, has already arrived for many. On farms in Ohio, Texas, and Nebraska, farmers use small computers in their homes to get current prices and market trends on commodities they plan to buy or sell.

At the same time farmers are checking their markets, a stock broker on the California coast may be checking stock prices with a computer connected to the television in his den, and a precious metals trader in Denver is using hers to get the Zurich and London gold and silver prices. In Manitoba, a student programmer uses his home computer to call up the big university computer and do his programming assignment for the week (thus avoiding driving to the computer center in a blizzard), and in Massachusetts a secretary uses a home computer to "talk" to the computer in the office where she works. She gets typing assignments that way, does the work on her computer, and then transmits the complete assignment back to the office printer via a phone connection to her computer. The secretary saves time, the expense of car pools and baby sitters, and doesn't have to fight rush hour traffic every day.

The farmer, the stock broker, the trader, the student programmer, and the secretary all use the computer for two reasons. First, they get the information they need quickly, and second, they save time and effort. A third benefit for many computer owners is convenience. In some sections of the country, computers in the home are used to check on airline reservations, pay bills, look at movie reviews, shop for catalog merchandise, get detailed weather forecasts, and display information and ads from local or out-of-town newspapers. In the near future you will be able to go shopping by sitting down at your computer and selecting the items you want to purchase. You may even be able to compare prices in nearby stores without spending time and money driving to each store.

First time buyers of computers are often unaware of the many potential uses of a computer as a communications device. Many current owners, however, use their computer regularly as a communications system, and the future is likely to bring a tremendous increase as new services become available.

Terms such as *electronic mail, teleconferencing, networks* and *information management* are tossed about regularly today. When you finish reading this chapter, you will know what those terms actually mean and you will know how to use your computer as a communications device.

There are actually two ways that computers communicate with other computers. Many current applications use ordinary telephone lines to provide the link between your computer and another system. Actually *line* is probably a misnomer since today most long distance phone calls are transmitted via land based microwave systems or by satellite. We will use the term *phone line* to denote any of the newfangled technology. The principle is still the same and the monthly bill still comes from the phone company.

In addition to systems that use the ordinary telephone, a few use cable television wires as a means of interconnection. Most of the examples in this chapter will take advantage of *Ma Bell's* technology, but more and more cities are adding cable services that can be connected to a personal computer.

Five major uses come to mind when we think of the computer as a communications device:

Information Management – The computer can allow us to tap into all sorts of *electronic information banks* where data we want is sorted and stored. A doctor can check for information on a new disease; a professor can find foundations that give money for research in a particular area, and a consumer can locate a store that sells a particular item or brand; a student can access reports on various subjects.

One of the earliest of the information utilities was the Prestel system developed and marketed in London by the British Post Office. There are some efforts to bring the British system to the U.S. as a commercial product, but Prestel is probably too expensive to become popular here. The special equipment required costs over $1000 and is not as versatile as a small computer that costs less. The Prestel system may be cost effective in Britain because of the limitations in British phones. U.S. systems tend to use small computers such as the ATARI 400 or ATARI 800 Computer instead, and to communicate over ordinary phone lines.

Electronic Mail and Electronic Publishing – Members of most *networks* can write messages to other members. Each time a person connects to the service it will indicate whether there are messages for the member. The term electronic mail refers to this service. It is the ability to use a computer or terminal to send information to someone else, thus bypassing the U.S. Postal Service in the process. In addition, there are numerous electronic bulletin boards or newsletters which contain special types of information. Network members, for example, who own a particular computer may be able to read notes and articles about their computer.

PCNET (Personal Computer Network, People's Computer Company, Menlo Park, California) is one attempt to develop a system for relaying messages you type in to various parts of the country. Another project, Electronic Information Exchange System (EIES) is an experimental project developed by Murray Turoff and Starr Roxanne Hiltz at the New Jersey Institute of Technology in Newark, New Jersey. It is more appropriately described as a *teleconferencing* project rather than just as *electronic mail.* EIES is intended to serve as a channel of communication for scientists in various parts of the country who are working on similar projects. Comments, critiques, and descriptions of new developments can be typed into the system from a keyboard located in the scientist's laboratory. Later, researchers can sit in front of their own computers and read what other scientists have input. In addition, there is the possibility of getting groups of scientists together by phone so they can interact *on line.*

Consumer Services – Imagine touching a few keys on your ATARI 800 Home Computer and making all your travel arrangements yourself at any hour of the day or night. A student can access a needed government publication at home at 2:00 a.m. when the paper is due at 8:00 a.m. Can you conceive of being able to access the latest newswire or stock report at the same time the editor of your newspaper does? How would you like to read movie reviews or pro-football statistics on your screen? Visualize the excitement of immediately announcing a new baby to your friends all over the country by typing a few words. Imagine how much fun Christmas shopping could be if you didn't have to fight the crowds in the stores but could view products on your television screen and just press a few keys to order them.

Imagine what it would be like, if you could do all these things and more. Well, you can. A few lucky residents in Columbus, Ohio can now access all of these services, or will be able to in the near future. These individuals are participating in a test project jointly conducted by Atari, Inc., CompuServe Inc. (a time sharing computer information service company), and Qube (a cable television subsidiary of Warner Amex Cable Communication).

One of the greatest wonders of this new system is that you don't need any technical knowledge to use it. Instructions for using this system are presented in nontechnical language via a cable network. The instructions are similar to educational television with one big difference. Viewers type information on their Qube console and interact directly with the instructor. To access the wealth of information available from CompuServe Information Service, they merely call up an index of the information services and touch the designated key for the information they wish to see. You, too, can access some of these services from CompuServe Information Services with your ATARI Personal Computer, although not via cable. All you need is an ATARI 830™ Acoustic Modem, an ATARI 850™ Interface Module, the TELELINK™ I cartridge and a standard telephone. Then you can sign up for the services from CompuServe or other service companies. Why is the Columbus project so revolutionary? First of all, this is the first time cable communication has been linked with capabilities of a personal computer system, resulting in a total home information and entertainment system. The possibilities are almost limitless. Cable transmissions of information can provide fast and inexpensive transmission throughout the country. Two-way cable systems will let you communicate directly with an information source. This opens opportunities for educational studies, viewer participation in panels and shows, research and lots of other things that no one has even thought of yet.

Shopping by computer and paying bills by computer are two examples of consumer applications. There is a wide range of consumer services available now, but this is only a sampling of what will be available in the future.

Experimental projects currently underway allow some computer owners to sit at home and pay their bills by computer. One popular system to be discussed later in this chapter (THE SOURCE, AMERICA'S INFORMATION UTILITY) plans a service called The Music Source which will let you select any of over 5000 records or tapes which are then charged to your credit card and delivered by UPS.

There are even rumors that THE SOURCE, AMERICA'S INFORMATION UTILITY, will establish an educational program by which students can earn an MBA degree from an accredited university. Students would get lectures and assignments on their computer display. Most of the work for the degree could thus be accomplished at home.

Downloading Programs – Some services provide a list of computer programs available to users. If you want to buy one of the programs, the service will transmit (*download*) the program to your computer and bill you for the cost of the program at the end of the month. Once it is in the memory of your computer it is possible to make a copy of the program on a cassette tape or disk. Although this feature has been discussed and talked about for several years, there are really very few programs that can be downloaded at present.

Computing – It may seem redundant to say a computer can be used for computing, but this is a little different. One advantage of small computers is that they can be used by themselves (e.g. as *standalone* systems), but there may be times when you need to use the computing power of a gigantic 5 million dollar computer. Most of us can't afford to buy such a machine, but a small computer in our home or office will allow us to connect to a big *mainframe* computer and use its computing power for a nominal charge.

In the next section of this chapter we will discuss in more detail some specific services available today. The two national networks, which will be discussed first, offer many different types of services. Other, more specialized or limited services will be discussed in the final sections of the chapter.

PERSONAL COMPUTER NETWORKS

Currently there are two established, national, general purpose networks: THE SOURCE, AMERICA'S INFORMATION UTILITY, and CompuServe. Both can be used by anyone with a small computer, a credit card (so they can bill you monthly), and a telephone. The only special equipment required is a device called a *modem*. It allows you to connect the computer to the telephone line and transmit as well as receive information over the phone. Calls to the two major networks are local calls in many major cities. (If you live in a smaller city or in a rural area, there may be additional charge for each minute of *connect time*.)

The Source Telecomputing Corporation

THE SOURCE, AMERICA'S INFORMATION UTILITY is a service of Source Telecomputing Corporation, 1616 Anderson Road, McLean, Virginia 22102 (800-336-3366). The Source began in 1979, and in 1980 the Reader's Digest Corporation bought controlling interest in THE SOURCE. With a company that big behind it, service should be quite good.

A person wanting to sign up with THE SOURCE can do so through the mail or at many computer stores. Like cable television, there is an initial hookup charge. The charge is $100. After that, THE SOURCE charges $5.75 per off peak hour (6pm-12am) weekdays, $4.25 per hour 12am-7am weekdays, all day weekends and holidays and $18 per hour during prime time (7am-6pm weekdays). There is a minimum monthly charge of $10 whether you use the system or not. The phone call to THE SOURCE is a local call in over 300 cities. What do you get for your money? One answer comes from Ken Skier in his article on THE SOURCE (*On Computing*, Summer, 1981), "In the world's biggest candy store, which aisle do you explore first?" While thinking of THE SOURCE as a candy store may require a bit of poetic license, you can easily think of it as a communications supermarket.

Few people will want every service offered by THE SOURCE, but it's nice to know the services are there. Some of the most interesting services are described below:

Consumer Services – With THE SOURCE, you can check airline schedules worldwide and make hotel, car rental, and airline reservations. There is a classified ad bulletin board where you can check for bargains from all across the country (or sell a bargain yourself). In addition, there is a discount buying service that lets you select brand name products from the service and pay for them with your Visa or Mastercard. Finally, there is a real estate service that helps you buy or sell a house.

THE SOURCE for its time has been an amazing service and one that would have been impossible only a few years ago.

Computing Services – THE SOURCE allows you to write and run programs in a variety of languages including BASIC, COBOL, and FORTRAN, among others. THE SOURCE also has quite a few *canned* programs of their own which are available for use. Many are free; some involve a small charge. The programs available include games, business programs such as accounts payable, and programs for special applications such as statistical analysis of large amounts of data. You cannot buy these programs. In essence you *rent* them by connecting to THE SOURCE.

Data Bases – A service likely to be used by many subscribers is access to some of the many data bases available via THE SOURCE. One of the more popular data bases is the United Press International (UPI) wire service. It is possible to tell THE SOURCE to put the UPI output on the screen and watch the news scroll by. However, that is a very inefficient way of finding the news you're interested in. From your computer you can tell the UPI data base exactly which stories you want to read. A subscriber who wants to get the results of a local referendum in a distant city or read stories about a particular corporation's plans for a merger can instruct THE SOURCE to locate and display any news stories filed recently with UPI that fit your requirements. The computer is not likely to replace your daily newspaper; it is easier to read the news in a newspaper than on a television screen (and probably cheaper). On the other hand, when you read the newspaper, you are reading only the news that was selected by the editor down at the paper. If you want to follow a specific story, the UPI data base can be used to find and read stories that never appeared in your local paper. In addition, even if a UPI story does appear in your local paper it will probably be an edited version. A 300 line UPI story may become a 30 line article in the paper. By getting the story directly from UPI, you get all the information provided by UPI, instead of an edited version.

The UPI data base is only one of a large number available on THE SOURCE. It may take some effort to learn how to use them effectively, but the effort is worth it to people who want to keep abreast of a particular news topic. Other data bases include the New York Times-News Summary, and a consumer information data base also from the New York Times.

Electronic Mail – If you want to send a message or letter to another subscriber to THE SOURCE, you can type it in on your keyboard and store it in the memory of THE SOURCE's computers. The next time that subscriber signs on, THE SOURCE will signal there is a message waiting. It is even possible to call a toll free number and dictate a letter over the phone. Your letter will be put in the electronic mail file.

Special-interest groups can also use the electronic mail feature by placing information in a sort of electronic bulletin board that can be read by subscribers with similar interests.

For example, Atari, Inc. might have a bulletin board that only ATARI Home Computer owners can access.

CompuServe

The major competitor to THE SOURCE is CompuServe Information Service (now owned by H & R Block), originally known as MicroNET. There are many similarities between the two and some differences. CompuServe charges only $30 initially, and charges $5 per hour during non prime time (6pm to 5:30am weekdays, all day weekends and holidays). With the purchase of the ATARI TeleLink I or TeleLink II cartridge, there is no sign-up fee. CompuServe is not available during normal working hours since the company that runs this service uses its computers to serve commercial customers during that time. The connect call is local in over 260 cities.

CompuServe offers services similar to those of THE SOURCE. One nice feature of CompuServe is the ATARI Newsletter available to subscribers. You can dial CompuServe and read all sorts of information about ATARI Computers. CompuServe has a good reputation for reliability and fast response times. Instead of UPI, CompuServe uses the Associated Press news wire (as well as the New York Times service). CompuServe also offers information on topics as diverse as home repair, personal health, and recipes. Like THE SOURCE, it has book and movie reviews available as well as a sports information service. There is even a file of *computer art* that can be copied on your printer, if you have one.

Again, like THE SOURCE, CompuServe has a number of financial data bases available.

Chooseing between THE SOURCE and CompuServe is a hard choice. You may want to use both services. They offer something unique and you can probably afford both. The CompuServe package can be conveniently purchased at many computer dealers or from CompuServe (P.O. Box 20212, Columbus, Ohio 43220, 800-848-8990).

Other Data Bases

In addition to the general purpose information supermarkets, there are many specialized services which offer a more limited range of services. What they lack in breadth, however, is more than offset by the depth of some of these services. Some financial services, for example, won't have any

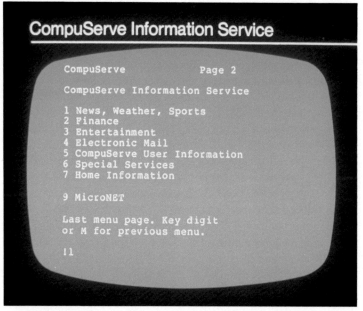

The CompuServe menu gives you a number of options.
The CompuServe menu can even give you a menu.

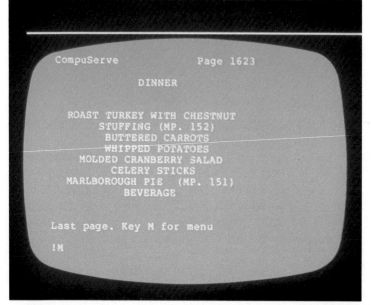

A home computer, a telephone and a modem with interface together give you access to many data bases, including the Dow Jones News/Retrieval Service.

information on the weekend football games, but they can provide detailed information on the performance of thousands of U.S. and foreign corporations. Current stock prices and stock performance patterns are only a starting point. There is *deep background* information that covers the corporate history as well as recent news items relating to the corporation's products, management policies, merger possibilities, and technological status.

One information service available for ATARI Computers is the Dow Jones News/Retrieval Service. With the DOW JONES* New/Retrieval Service, your ATARI Computer can provide current quotations on stocks, bonds, mutual funds, and treasury bills. Your computer can display current news items related to your investments.

There are too many data bases to even list all of them here. Many are very specialized and very expensive (as much as $85,000 per year plus connect time charges!). One source of additional information is the *Directory of On-Line Data Bases* ($60 a year for four issues) which is available in some libraries or from Cuadra Associates, Inc., 1523 Sixth Street, Suite 12, Santa Monica, California 90401. Another source of information that may be easier (and cheaper) to get is an article in the April 1981 issue of *Creative Computing* entitled "A Guide to Data Banks." In the next section we will discuss one of the largest and most widely used data banks now in service.

Dialog

Graduate students and professors in many academic disciplines have used Dialog, a subsidiary of Lockheed Missile and Space Company (Lockheed Information Systems, 3460 Hillview Avenue, Palo Alto, California 94304, 415-858-2700). Most major universities offer Dialog services through their libraries, but individuals can also subscribe to the service and be billed monthly. If you only use Dialog occasionally you may find it easier to go to the library and get a specially trained librarian to talk to Dialog on your behalf. Dialog uses a rather complicated but powerful system of instructions to find exactly the information you need.

---

*Trademark of Dow Jones & Company, Inc.

Dialog is not really one data base, it is over 75. There are data bases for chemists, patent attorneys, philosophers, special education teachers, anthropologists, physicians, and many, many others. When you talk to Dialog, one of the first things it wants to know is which data base you need to use. A special educator, for example, might use ERIC while a psychologist would use the Psychological Abstracts data base.

Once that is determined, you can tell Dialog exactly what is desired. A simple example would be a special education teacher who wants to know about reading programs for emotionally disturbed elementary school age children. Using ERIC it would be possible to tell Dialog to find articles about reading programs but to include only those articles about emotionally disturbed elementary school children. Dialog then searches through thousands of references in its ERIC files and tells you how many it found. Suppose there are 465 articles and papers from 1971 to the present. If that is too many, you can make the search more specific (e.g. only reading programs that involve phonics training) or limit the years searched (e.g. only 1979 to 1982).

As you work with Dialog it is possible to bring up abstracts of the articles on the screen to see if they indeed cover the topics of interest. Abstracts and references of relevant articles can then be copied on your printer if you have one, or Dialog will print out the results of any search you do and mail it to you. The printer used by Dialog is fast, and produces very readable output. It generally takes no more than a few days to receive printouts.

Dialog is not cheap. Connect time charges depend on the database used, but range around $50 per hour. Each *hit* or abstract printed usually costs between 5 and 10 cents. It is possible, however, to save several days in the library reference room by spending 45 minutes on Dialog.

Local Computer Networks

In addition to the nationally available information supermarkets, there are hundreds of local networks run by universities and colleges, computer clubs, amateur radio clubs, and special interest groups. These networks allow a member (or in some cases, anyone who knows the phone number) to call a number and interact with the network's computer. Some systems limit use to reading the local electronic bulletin board, others actually allow access to the programming power of a large computer system from the comfort of your home. Check with your local computer store for information on what is available in your area.

Chapter 6

Buying A Communications Computer

A fast and easy way to get into communications is the ATARI kit, THE COMMUNICATOR™. It consists of TELELINK™ I (a terminal program for the ATARI Computers), the ATARI 850 Interface Module, and the ATARI 830 Acoustic Modem. You can use either the ATARI 800 Computer or ATARI 400 Computer with this package and it has everything you need to get started. Atari, Inc. evens includes one free hour of connect time on several of the more popular services.

Of the seven steps to buying a computer described in Chapter 2 only two, Software Considerations and Minimum Requirements/Preferred Features will be dealt with here since they are the only ones that call for special consideration when buying a communications computer.

SOFTWARE CONSIDERATIONS

A computer must have a set of instructions to follow before it can act as a terminal. The term *terminal* refers to any device that can be used to *talk* to a remotely located computer. You can buy a terminal whose only function is to allow you to communicate with a computer by phone. Most people, however, prefer to spend their money on a computer, because it can be used as a terminal, but has many other uses as well.

A terminal program can be obtained in several different ways. Some manufacturers offer an optional cassette which contains the program needed to make the computer work as a terminal. Several vendors offer *superterminal* packages on cassette or disk that turn a particular brand of computer into a smart terminal. The cost of these packages varies from around $15 to $400 depending on the sophistication of the program and the price of competing programs.

One of the least expensive ways to get a terminal program for the ATARI Computers is to buy the February, 1981 issue of the magazine, *Compute!*. A short little program on page 75 by Henrique Veludo is written in ATARI BASIC and can be typed into the computer in less than five minutes. Although Veludo is correct when he describes it as "a short, unsophisticated program," it is an easy way to experiment with the idea. You will need an ATARI 830 Acoustic Modem and the ATARI 850 Interface Module.

A more comprehensive terminal program is TELELINK I from Atari. It is a very good terminal program. It has a number of very nice features that make the ATARI 400 Computer or ATARI 800 Computer easy to use as a terminal. George Blank wrote a very nice article entitled "Hooking Up with ATARI" in the April, 1981 issue of *Creative Computing*. After taking a few well placed jabs at one of the larger manufacturers for producing shoddy serial I/O boards, he goes on to praise the ATARI Computer program and describe his use of TELELINK I to access CompuServe Information Services.

TELELINK I comes in a cartridge just like many of the ATARI Computer games. With the cartridge installed, turning on the computer causes the program to be loaded into the computer's memory automatically. Then, assuming the ATARI 850 Interface Module and modem are connected, you can call up a computer and talk.

TELELINK I is not the most sophisticated terminal program available (nor is it the most expensive), but it does have several useful commands. TELELINK I supports a printer that can be used to make printed copies of the material that appears on your television screen. That can be very useful. As more and more ATARI Computers reach the hands of users, expect to see more sophisticated terminal programs (e.g. programs that allow you to store data on disk or cassette).

MINIMUM REQUIREMENTS/PREFERRED KEY FEATURES

Display Characteristics – Every major small computer available today uses either a television or a video monitor as a display screen. The format used to display information on the screen however, varies considerably. The ATARI 400 and 800 Computers, for example, can display 24 lines of 40 characters each. That is a total of 960 characters on the screen at one time. Other computers in the under $1000 range also use the 24 by 40 format, 16 lines of 62 characters, or 16 lines of 32 characters. More expensive computers generally display 24 lines of 80 characters.

In principle, the more characters on the screen at once, the easier it is to use the computer. There are some catches, however. Computers like the ATARI 800 Computer and ATARI 400 Computer can display in color and are designed to be used with standard color televisions. Color televisions will not display a clean 80 character line. The options then are to have fewer characters on the screen at one time and thus be able to use a regular television or increase the cost of the system and include a color monitor.

Since good color monitors are very expensive, many manufacturers have elected to keep the cost of their product down and offer display patterns that can be handled by the Stromberg-Carlson in the den. Most of the more popular network systems will work nicely with a computer that puts 24 lines of 40 characters on the screen. Some, particularly business and university time-sharing systems, insist on sending everything to you in 80 character lines. At Texas Tech, we can tell the main computer how many characters are to be put in each line. You should be sure your *host* computer is that agreeable before buying a particular computer for communications.

A second factor to consider is the type of material that can be displayed on the screen. Some computers handle only upper case or capital letters; others accept both upper and lower case; still others accept upper and lower case letters as well as many different types of graphics symbols. Currently most mainframe computer networks function with upper-case-only computers as terminals, but you may not be able to take

FROM: CHICAGO, IL
TO: ONTARIO, CA

DEPART APT ARRIVE APT FLIGHT
CLASS DAYS   MEALS PLANE STOPS
0700A   0   1141A   Q   W 4181
FY8M 1234567   B   B   D10 0
0745A   0   1155A   L   TW 0075
        1234567   B   B   747 0
0915A   0   0111P   L   TW 0201
FY   1234567   B   B   707 0
0915A   0   0111P   L   7A7 0
FY   1234567   L   L   UA 0211
1010A   0   1155A   L   725 0
FY8M 1234567   L   L   UA 0647
1010A   0   0212P   L   L   UA 0101
FY8M 1234567   LLL   L   747 0
1140A   0   0119P   L   L   UA 0102
        1234567   L   L   747 0

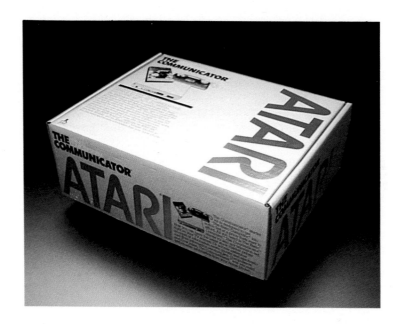

HOME COMMUNICATIONS SYSTEM

The ATARI Home Computer provides you with easy access to travel information at home through THE SOURCE, AMERICA'S INFORMATION UTILITY.

advantage of all the features. When the price is the same, buy the computer with the most display options (e.g. upper case, lower case, graphics).

Serial Interface – The actual connection between the computer and the network is via a *serial I/O* port. Just what that cryptic phrase means is explained in Chapter 12. Here, it is only important to know that a computer must have a serial output port to function as a communications computer. Some computers come with a serial port as standard equipment. Others offer it as an option which can be purchased if needed. Many printers also connect to the computer through the serial port.

The ATARI Computers do not have a serial port as standard equipment. There are, however, four serial ports in the optional ATARI 850 Interface Module. This module also includes one parallel I/O port (also explained in Chapter 12).

Be careful when comparing serial I/O ports. When a salesperson says a computer has a serial port ask three questions:

1. What baud rates will it accept?
2. Will it run full duplex?
3. Can it function in an auto answer mode?

Here is what those questions mean. The *baud* rate is the speed at which the computer can send and receive information through its serial port. A rate of 300 baud corresponds to a little less than 30 characters a second. Most networks are designed to receive and transmit data at 300 baud, but some run at 1200 baud (four times as fast). Connections that involve using ordinary long-distance phone circuits generally use 300 baud. As you might expect, it is essential that the computer be able to handle 300 baud and it would be nice if it accepted other speeds as well. (Printers that are connected to the serial ports may run as slow as 60 and as high as 1200 baud). The serial ports on the ATARI 850 Interface Module run at 60, 66, 75, 100, 110, 134.5, 150, 300, 600, 1200, 1800, 2400, 4800, and 9600 baud. If you have something that runs at another baud rate, we've never heard of it. The rates Atari selected cover everything from World War II surplus Teletype machines to modems for use on high-speed leased phone lines.

Now what about the term *full duplex?* Some systems require the computers on each end of the network to take turns. That is, when one is talking the other can only listen. The connection doesn't allow a computer to talk and listen at the same time. That is called *half duplex*. When using a system that is half duplex you have to wait until the computer on the other end finishes before you can talk to it. While that may seem like a polite and civilized way to talk to a computer, it can actually lead to problems. Suppose you mistakenly give the computer you're connected to an instruction that causes it to start doing something that may take hours to do (e.g. listing the train schedules for Italy and Yugoslavia) when you really wanted something else (e.g. the schedule for the Milan to Belgrade express). It would be nice to be able to let the computer know you really don't want everything it is dutifully sending you. Look for a computer that can handle full duplex communication. At a minimum the computer should be capable of sending a true BREAK signal out the serial port. BREAK is a signal many systems use to tell the computer on the other end to stop whatever it is doing and wait for further instructions. Technically a true BREAK signal involves sending a +5 volt signal to the modem for just under half a second. We have one $4000 computer that has a break key displayed prominently on its keyboard and a fancy set of programs that supposedly turn it into a super smart terminal. Unfortunately, the programmer and designers forgot to program the break key to send a BREAK signal, and the computer is useless as a terminal unless you modify it. There are several computers that have break keys but no BREAK signal.

Finally, let's deal with the *auto answer* question. This is really a luxury rather than a requirement, but it is a nice luxury. The standard way to connect to a network is to dial the correct number and listen for a high pitched tone that signals the network is ready to receive data. The phone is then placed in two sponge rubber cups on top of the modem and the connection is made. Then you can type instructions on your keyboard and a computer thousands of miles away will understand and follow them.

When you call another computer and it puts the high pitched tone on the phone line, it is working in an *auto answer mode*. That is, the computer answers the phone and sets up to receive instructions without requiring human assistance. If you want to be able to call and talk to your own computer from a remote location or use it to run a local network for a local club or interest group, you will need the auto answer capability.

The Modem – A modem (short for *modulator/demodulator*) converts the electrical signals from the computer into tones which are transmitted over ordinary phone lines. On the other end of the connection another modem converts the tones it hears back into electrical signals the computer can understand. A few years ago, it was possible to buy a used modem for as little as $50, but as more and more computer owners learned about all the nice things you can do with a modem, the used equipment was quickly snapped up.

There are still kits that provide you with all the parts needed for a modem. Unless you have experience building with integrated circuits and soldering tiny, heat sensitive parts on a circuit board, we advise you to buy an assembled unit. That advice is particularly valid these days because several inexpensive modems are now available. Several manufacturers sell modems for prices between $150 and $275. All modems are not created equal, however.

A modem can be a half duplex or full duplex model. A half duplex modem can listen (receive) and transmit but not at the same time. A full duplex modem can transmit and receive at the same time. You want a full duplex modem because it can be switched to half duplex when required. Modems can also be *answer, originate,* or *answer and originate.* These terms require a little explaining. When an answer modem is told to send a *1* out, it sends a 2225Hz tone; it sends a 2025Hz tone when it is told to send a *0.* Each letter and number has a code, much like the telegrapher's Morse code, with *1*'s and *0*'s replacing the *dits* and *dahs.* The code for a capital *A* for example is 1000001. A modem converts this code into a pattern of tones to transmit them over the phone. There is, however, a slight twist in the plot. Answer modems transmit tones in the 2000 Hz range, but they do not receive tones in that range. They *listen* for two tones – a 1270 Hz tone that stands for a *1* and a 1070 Hz tone that stands for a *0.* The different receive and transmit tones are necessary to keep the modem from receiving its own transmissions.

Now what about the originate modems? As you might expect, originate modems receive the tones transmitted by answer modems and transmit the tones answer modems receive. Thus two answer or two originate modems can't talk to each other. If you have a friend in Pocatello, with an ATARI Computer, your computers can only talk to each other if one has an answer modem and the other has an originate modem. Most networks have an answer modem, so you should at least get an originate modem. The best option, however, is to get a modem that can be used in either answer or originate modes. They cost more, but are more versatile. The ATARI 830 Acoustic Modem has a switch that allows you to change from answer to originate.

One final comment about modems. They are also rated with regard to the highest speed (BAUD rate) which can be used with them. Almost all the modems used on small computers are rated up to 300 BAUD. Commercial modems that reliably transmit and receive at very high BAUD rates are also very expensive. Buy one only if you really need the capability. Be sure, if you want to use a faster modem that your computer, the phone line, and the computer you want to talk to can also use the higher speed.

SUMMARY: THE COMMUNICATIONS PACKAGE

As we mentioned at the beginning of this chapter the ATARI kit, THE COMMUNICATOR contains all the accessories you need to use your ATARI Computer as a communications computer. Regardless of how you use your communications computer, at some point you will probably want to add a printer and a disk drive. With THE COMMUNICATOR, you can enter one of the most exciting and useful areas of personal computer applications.

for its willingness to embrace new technology (some suggest we are still trying to deal with the printing press and moveable type.) And when education has accepted technology, the promises made by the technocrats have rarely, if ever, been fulfilled. Educational television is a good example from our recent past. It did not revolutionize education as promised; it is a tool that is sometimes useful in accomplishing some educational goals.

Many experienced teachers can list at least ten *new* ideas or new technologies that were supposed to revolutionize education. Yet teachers still teach in much the same way they did 30 years ago. You can understand why educators aren't rushing to embrace this new computer technology.

In spite of the reasons why we won't see a revolution in education, there is good reason to expect that education will evolve or change rather quickly during the next ten years. We feel there are two main thrusts that will bring more change in the next decade than has occurred in the last 50 years.

THE DESCHOOLING OF LEARNING

For most of the twentieth century, education has been institutionalized. Learning is something children do in a classroom supervised by one or more adults. The traditional school will not disappear, but before the end of this century it will likely play a much smaller role than it does today. More people will spend a significant amount of time learning at home, in the office, the factory, and at adult learning centers. Increasingly, our society is viewing learning as a lifelong task rather than something children do to prepare for adulthood. That view is being accepted today because we live in a time of accelerated change. Information is outdated quickly; new information seems to appear at a faster and faster rate. Secretaries must learn to deal with *word processors,* office machine repair personnel see more electronic calculators and fewer mechanical adding machines in their shops and factory workers have to learn about industrial robots. It's hard to find the mainspring in a digital watch and even more difficult to find the pilot light on a microwave oven.

The point is, we must continue to learn, regardless of our age, if we are to cope with the demands of life today, and that

Educational programs are a good supplement to classroom learning.➡

learning must occur someplace other than the classrooms where we spent the fourth grade. Fortunately, the small computer came along at a time when it can be particularly helpful in both traditional and non-traditional learning environments.

THE SMALL COMPUTER AS A LEARNING MACHINE

Computers have been used in education for at least 20 years. Pioneering projects such as Suppes' work at Stanford University, however, used large, expensive computers which could not be placed in individual classrooms or resource centers. Instead, a keyboard/printer device, called a terminal, was placed in the school and connected to the computer by phone. This method was the only option available 15 years ago, and it is still a major means of getting computer-based learning into the classroom. Control Data's PLATO project is a sophisticated system of computer-assisted learning, capable of teaching everything from preschool letter recognition to graduate level physics. Another commercial venture, Computer Curriculum Corporation, uses large computers to distribute their educational programs to several hundred school systems.

In spite of the history of large computers as learning machines, we feel the future of educational computing lies in the increased use of small computers. They are cheaper, easier to use, more reliable, and easier to install in a school. When faced with the choice of buying one large computer or 100 small computers, school districts now frequently elect to buy small computers such as the ATARI Computers.

Individuals who buy a computer generally don't have a choice, they can only afford to buy a small computer. Why, however, are schools leaning toward tabletop computers? Cost is one reason. The small computers often cost less than the price of one terminal for one of the larger systems. Dependability is probably the second major reason. To use a time-sharing system (i.e. terminal in classroom, computer elsewhere) requires a terminal that is working, a phone line that is reasonably clear of interference, and a remotely located computer (sometimes several hundred miles away) that is not only working but has the time to respond quickly to the student at the terminal. If any one of the elements in the chain isn't working, the entire system doesn't work and the teacher loses a scheduled learning period. The logistics involved in using small computers are much less involved and therefore inherently more reliable.

A distinguished computer educator put the point very clearly in a recent article: "The inexpensive microcomputer, more than any other event, has made school-based computer education a possibility. The development of small time-sharing systems about ten years ago brought hardware costs per student terminal down to about $10,000 – a major breakthrough, but still far too costly for most schools. Worse yet, time-sharing systems lack robustness against hardware failure: 97% uptime is achievable and sounds good, but it means that there is no computer one day per month, and no computer class. The new personal computers have brought the cost down to from $1000 to $2000 and have increased robustness dramatically: 97% uptime for personal computers means that out of a collection of ten machines, nine are working all the time and all ten are working most of the time. Class goes on." (A. Luehrmann, "Computer Illiteracy – A National Crisis and a Solution for It", *Byte*, July, 1980, 98-102)

Don't expect to see 35 ATARI 400 Computers in your fifth grader's classroom next year (although you might). The use of computers in traditional educational settings will increase tremendously in the next five years. Some companies appear to have made a corporate decision that their learning products will be purchased in larger quantities by parents than by schools. Products such as Speak and Spell*, Speak and Read*, and the Little Professor* calculator have all been marketed very successfully to parents. Some of the hand-held products have sold well to parents but not to schools. Although they are excellent learning aids, schools have accounted for only a small fraction of their sales. If you are interested in learning more about computer assisted learning you may want to read current issues of three very good computer oriented education magazines listed below:

The Computing Teacher (Computing Center, Eastern Oregon State College, La Grande, Oregon 97850). One of the oldest publications in the field, it carries a range of articles on uses of computers in elementary and high schools.

---

*Trademark of Texas Instruments

Educational Computer Magazine (P.O. Box 535, Cupertino, California 95015). Begun in 1981 this is a user oriented magazine designed primarily for educators who want to use computers in their schools. If early issues are any indication, it will be a very good publication.

Classroom Computer News (P.O. Box 266, Cambridge, Massachusetts 02138). Also begun in 1981, this publication uses a modified newspaper format and covers some of the same areas as *Educational Computer Magazine* but with more emphasis on the *news* in educational computing (e.g. which publishing company is coming out with new software and when).

Books of interest include *The Computer in the School: Tutor, Tool, Tutee* (Columbia University Press, 1981) which was edited by Robert P. Taylor. This book consists of a very good introductory chapter and reprints of articles by pioneers Alfred Bork, Thomas Dwyer, Arthur Luehrmann, Seymour Papert, and Patrick Suppes. Another book we recommend is *Using Computers in Education* by Willis, Johnson, and Dixon. The three authors are all professors in the College of Education at Texas Tech University. Their book, available from dilithium Press (P.O. Box 606, Beaverton, Oregon 97075), is an introduction to educational computing.

◄——*Teachers and students can be involved in several projects at once.*

Since the ATARI Computers generate sound, you can compose with the aid of a computer.

WHAT CAN COMPUTERS DO?

The focus of this section will be on what computers *can* do rather than what they *are* doing at present. Currently most public school students and many university students have no contact at all with a computer during their educational career. You can view computers in an educational setting in two general ways – as the focus of learning and as aids to the learning process. The concept of *computer literacy* incorporates the first view. Arthur Luehrmann, in an article in *Byte* (July, 1980, 98-102) made this observation:

"Computing plays such a crucial role in everyday life and in the technological future of this nation that the general public's ignorance of the subject constitutes a national crisis.

The ability to use computers is as basic and necessary to a person's formal education as reading, writing, and arithmetic. . .

Yet, despite computing's critical importance today, the overwhelming majority of this country's general public is woefully ill-prepared to live and work in the Age of Information as some have called it."

Luehrmann makes the point many people are making these days – the next generation will need to understand computers to understand their jobs. Even if computers could not be used to teach reading, math, and the other school subjects, they would be important as a subject to study in themselves. Several computer manufacturers have gone to considerable lengths to provide books, computer-aided learning programs, and audio-visual aids in the area of computer literacy. For example, Atari, Inc. also has materials which can be used in the classroom or at home to learn about computers and how to use them. THE PROGRAMMER kit, for instance, contains several training aids. The INVITATION TO PROGRAMMING™ series by Atari includes programs and workbooks that can be used in computer literacy classes. In addition Atari provides a teacher's guide with their computer language ATARI PILOT (with "turtle" graphics).

The second view of computers in education – the computer as an aid to learning other subjects – is, in our view, just as important as computer literacy. The computer, particularly the small computer, offers both educators and learners unique features, such as sound and graphics, that help both deal with the demands of an information oriented society.

As mentioned earlier, computers have been used in education for many years. Computers can teach many subjects efficiently, and free the teacher to provide more special instruction to students. Early efforts grew out of the work of mechanical teaching machines and programmed learning – two movements that gained strength in the late 50's and early 60's and then subsided as problems and difficulties in application overwhelmed early hopes for the new methods. Computers were seen as one way to get around some of the problems of the machines and programmed texts. Many programmed instruction books were boring. In addition, it was difficult to individualize instruction. Even if a student understood something the first time it was presented, the lesson might keep presenting it over and over. Or, if a student needed additional instruction to consolidate learning, the programmed instruction lesson might still go on to new material. Early computer-assisted instruction did solve some of the problems common in programmed instruction but it also created new ones (e.g. reliability and costs), and it was not accepted or used by even a large minority of the teachers and professors.

Reliability and cost factors are not the problems they were then. Small computers that run most of the time and cost less than $1000 have attracted the interest of several school systems. There are even a few major educational computing efforts at the state or provincial level. Funded by a forward looking legislature, the Minnesota Educational Computing Consortium is one of the oldest and most successful projects. MECC began with the idea of using a large time-sharing computer that would be accessed from schools over phone lines. In recent years, however, their focus has shifted to the use of small computers. Some of MECC's educational software is now marketed nationally. Newer projects using small computers are underway in Alaska, Texas, and British Columbia. Computers are being used to teach skills as well as art, music, and creative writing. There is even a special language called PILOT which was designed specifically for educational computing. The Atari version of PILOT is an easy-to-use language that even young students can learn as their first com-

Small children can learn to draw graphics.

puter language. It is also a very functional language for educators who want to write their own educational programs.

A unique feature of ATARI PILOT is the inclusion of *Turtle Graphics* which were developed by Professor Seymour Papert at MIT. Turtle graphics allow children (and adults) to teach the computer to create and display animated color pictures. Much of Papert's work is based on the theories of Swiss psychologist Jean Piaget. Papert feels that if you allow children to work with computers, it will help in the development of their cognitive skills. His book, *Mindstorms*, presents his current thinking on computers, learning and children.

With features like turtle graphics, ATARI PILOT is likely to be a very popular language for educational applications. It should also gain in popularity as a first computer language. It is currently used in classes at Lawrence Hall of Science and in several other computer literacy projects.

Computer Assisted Instruction (CAI), Computer Aided Instruction (CAI), and Computer Assisted Learning (CAL) are all terms in general use that refer to the use of a computer in education. Although some authors have tried to give specific meanings to each term they are usually used interchangeably. Several more terms such as Computer Managed Instruction, Drill and Practice (D&P), and Simulation refer to specific types of computer aided learning. In this final section of the chapter we will provide some definitions of these terms and give examples of programs that aid learning.

DRILL AND PRACTICE

The simplest type of computer assisted instruction is drill and practice. D&P doesn't really teach you anything, it just gives you practice in something you learned in some other way. A common drill and practice program would be one that gives the student practice using basic math skills. A crude program for addition, for example, would randomly select two numbers to be added, display the problem on the screen, and wait for the student to type in an answer. If the answer is correct, another problem is presented; an incorrect answer usually means the computer will ask the student to try again. Two errors in a row means the student is given the answer. The computer then continues to give problems to be solved.

Several of the educational programs available from Atari are drill and practice exercises. One, STATES & CAPITALS, asks the student to name each of the states and their capitals. When run, it displays a color map of the United States on the screen and outlines the shape of a particular state (in the correct map location). The student then types in the name of the state and its capital. That state then changes color and another state's outline is added to the screen. The computer then waits for another response. For most of us, learning the location and names of states was boring drudgery at best. The computer, with its color display and challenge, makes it fun. When all 50 states have been added to the map on the screen, the computer prints out the number of states and capitals the student got right and how many were missed. Atari has a similar program called EUROPEAN COUNTRIES & CAPITALS.

A more sophisticated drill and practice program is TOUCH TYPING from Atari. It has several levels of practice and a number of sophisticated features. The Beginning Typing level gives the student practice on individual letters which are presented in groups of five. If you are a total beginner, the program starts by drilling you on the typing of A S D F and G which are the *home* keys for the left hand. You progress through all the letters, numbers, and punctuation symbols on the keyboard and then begin to type words or letter groups followed by sentences and paragraphs. The program keeps track of errors and identifies characters you're having trouble with; it times your work and prints out a speed in words per minute after an exercise; and it puts a color coded display of the keyboard on the screen while you're getting started. If you leave out a word during an exercise, the computer changes the color of the word missed. As you get more proficient the computer will remember troublesome words or letters and give you more practice on them. It is a friendly, convenient, effective way to learn touch typing. The ATARI 800 Computer keyboard is very similar to a typewriter keyboard, which means the skills you learn will help you use a regular typewriter, as well as the computer, more effectively.

Even fancier drill and practice programs select the difficulty level of problems on the basis of the students performance during earlier sessions; they remember errors and give the student extra practice and, if used in a school setting, they may provide the teacher with printouts of individual student and class progress. A well-known educational publisher, SRA (155 N. Wacker Drive, Chicago, Illinois 60606) markets a line of educational packages for the ATARI Computers and other machines, that includes drill and practice programs for addition, subtraction, multiplication, and division facts. When teachers and students use these programs, they can select the type and beginning difficulty level of problems. Once begun, the computer keeps track of the student's performance and moves on to more difficult problems when the student masters the current level. Drills can be timed if desired, so that students try to *beat the clock* and still get the correct answer. The programs keep track of students' performance and provide a printed record for the teacher. There are also several interesting games which the students get to play if they do well on their exercise. SRA's material is a bit more than a drill and practice program. For example, it uses the graphics features of the ATARI Computers to provide several types of *help* to students who don't quite understand how to do a problem.

SRA also has a program called PHONICS which runs on an ATARI Computer and is designed to be used in conjunction with a basal reading program for students in the primary grades.

In the coming months and years, there are likely to be thousands of drill and practice programs on a wide range of topics.

TUTORIAL PROGRAMS

A tutorial program does more than just give you practice on something you already know; it actually teaches. At the college level, the organization *Conduit* (Box 388, Iowa City, Iowa 52244) distributes a number of educational programs that run on small computers. There are programs that teach a student to apply Newton's Second Law and the Law of Gravitation to satellite orbits and another that teaches matrix algebra.

Many companies now offer tutorial programs for the ATARI 400 and 800 Computers. The Minnesota Educational Computing Consortium, one of the premier educational computing groups in the country, has developed an entire series of tutorial software for students in elementary and secondary schools. One distributor of educational software (Scholastic Microcomputer Instructional Materials, 904 Sylvan Avenue, Englewood Cliffs, New Jersey 07632), for example, offers programs that teach reading comprehension, vocabulary development, music, writing skills, and computer programming in BASIC. Another distributor (Opportunities for Learning, 8950 Lurline Avenue, Chatsworth, California 91311) markets programs such as Addition with Carrying, Fractions, Graphit, Quantitative Comparisons for the SAT, MECC Language Arts, Spelling Builder, Preschool IQ Builder, and Reading Comprehension. There are many tutorial programs available for the ATARI Computers.

ATARI also has a series of programs that teach conversational French, Spanish, German, or Italian. Designed for use in the home, the programs provide both audio and visual instruction. Words are pronounced and printed on the screen simultaneously. The language package comes complete with workbooks for drill and practice. Not only are these programs extremely useful for self study they could also be used in a language lab at a school.

Educational computer programs that use a tutorial format rather than a drill and practice method are much more difficult to write since you must teach the skill as well as evaluate learning. Still the number of tutorial programs is increasing rapidly. Several traditional educational publishers, in fact, are currently preparing tutorial software for many of the required subjects at the elementary and high school levels.

SIMULATIONS

We have a program called OREGON TRAIL that grabs the attention of both adults and children when it is used as a demonstration. OREGON TRAIL tells the group around the computer that they are on a wagon train leaving St. Joseph, Missouri for Oregon. The program allows the group to make decisions on how much food, bullets, medicine, and clothing to buy. They then select a wagon and oxen team, pay for them, and head for Oregon. Along the way the wagon train can run into all sorts of problems—floods, hostile riders, blizzards, broken wagons, and sickness. The settlers must decide how much food to eat each day, when to hunt, what to do when riders appear, and whether to stop and buy provisions at the forts along the way.

The decisions determine the likelihood of different types of problems occurring (e.g. eat poorly and you are more likely to become ill). While we have buried many a group of settlers along the trail to Oregon, some groups do make it through.

OREGON TRAIL is one of many simulations available today. A computer simulation puts the participant in a role and then requires decisions to be made that have consequences. Atari offers a simulation called KINGDOM™ that makes the player the ruler of an ancient city which has 1000 acres of land for cultivation, 100 citizens, and 3000 bushels of grain in storage. As ruler you must decide how much grain to give the people to eat, how much to save for seed, and how many acres to plant. Your decisions determine whether the kingdom starves or grows and develops (and requires more acres of grain next year).

Atari also has a more complicated simulation called ENERGY CZAR™ which strikes a little closer to home. The simulation is set in 1980 and you have been appointed Energy Czar by the President. You must manage the nation's energy resources while maintaining at least a reasonable level of acceptance in the public opinion polls. You get fired if less than 20% of the people think you are doing a good job and you become a NATIONAL HERO if at least 75% of those polled think you are doing a good job. The simulation is very complicated, you must make many decisions, and it requires you to keep track of many variables. A person who becomes a national hero will also learn a great deal about energy usage. The manual for ENERGY CZAR contains a considerable amount of information on energy use and management, as well as a list of references for more information.

Simulations are widely used in business and industry. Nuclear and chemical plant workers are trained by computer simulations. It is much less expensive to have a trainee blow up a make-believe plant on the screen than to make a real mistake while training in a real plant. Simulations are not only effective training tools, they are also fun. Many of the computer and arcade games that are so popular today are simulations designed for maximum enjoyment rather than as learning aids. The ATARI Computers are particularly suited to simulations because they have superior graphics capabilities and can generate a variety of sounds.

COMPUTER LITERACY AND ATARI PILOT

The concept of computer literacy has been mentioned several times in preceding chapters. Essentially, computer literacy involves acquiring an understanding of how computers work, what they can and cannot do, and some ability to use a computer. Many educators feel that computer literacy should be one of several important instructional goals in American education today. They base their view on the fact that computers are now used by people who work in thousands of different types of jobs, and on the likelihood that computer literacy will be a requirement for many more technical, professional, and service occupations in the future.

The ATARI Computers in many households are seen as an enjoyable and inexpensive way for parents and children alike to become computer literate. If literacy is one of the goals your family has in mind, you may want to consider purchasing the cartridge that allows your computer to understand ATARI PILOT. PILOT stands for *Programmed Inquiry, Learning, or Teaching.* This language was originally developed for educational applications. It was intended as a language teachers could learn quickly, and then use to write programs they could use in their classes. The ATARI version of PILOT is an excellent language for teachers and parents who want to write educational programs. ATARI PILOT is more than an educators language. It is now a popular *first language* for children and adults who are learning to program a computer for the first time. PILOT uses simple instructions and formats. You can be talking to your computer in PILOT in less than a day.

With PILOT's simplicity you might expect the language to be very limited, a "toy" language rather than a real computer language. Fortunately that is not true. In fact, PILOT is in some ways much more powerful than BASIC when it comes to handling words. (BASIC is better at working with numbers and math operations.) ATARI PILOT has instructions that allow you to take advantage of the color graphics features of the computer. It is also easy to write programs that include all sorts of sound effects. A unique feature of ATARI PILOT is the availability of *turtle graphics*, a form of graphics particularly suited for use with children. Some research studies, in fact, suggest that children who are exposed to an easy to learn and use language, incorporating features such as turtle graphics, may actually develop better thinking and problem solving skills.

ATARI PILOT comes with an instruction book designed for children. The school edition of the package includes a large manual for educators who wish to use it to write programs themselves and a delightfully illustrated student guide. Whether you are an educator looking for an easy to use language or a parent trying to decide which language should be the firstg one for your children, PILOT should be given serious consideration.

OTHER EDUCATIONAL APPLICATIONS

Computer literacy, drill and practice, tutorial programs, and simulations account for the greater majority of computer applications in education and learning today. Another approach, Computer Managed Instruction (CMI), uses the computer as a manager or overseer of learning. For example, students may be given a series of assignments that require them to read certain sections of a text and do some assignments in the library. As the student finishes each assignment he or she sits down at the computer and takes a test over the assignment. A pass means the student can go on to the next assignment, otherwise the computer provides suggestions for further study. CMI requires quite a bit of work from the teacher to arrange, but does not require the teacher to actually write programs that teach the student. In addition, CMI makes sense when computer presentation of the material is not feasible or not efficient (i.e. in a class on old English poetry). The computer can be used as an aid to learning if it does not actually do the teaching.

In the future, computers may be used to identify the learning or academic weaknesses of students through extensive diagnostic testing and to prescribe educational programs to meet a particular student's needs. They may also come to be considered useful tools in many classes much as calculators have. The future looks bright for educational computing whether it be in traditional classrooms or non-traditional settings such as the home.

In closing we refer you to Chapters 9 and 10 that deal with business applications. Many computers in schools play important roles as business computers as well. The same computer that is used in a typing or word processing class can be used in a class on accounting or business. There are several excellent financial programs, for example, for the ATARI Computers. Several schools we know of also use some of their educational computers in the office to prepare budgets, to keep track of accounts payable and to perform other routine business applications for the school.

Chapter 8

Selecting an Educational Computer

Can you see how a computer can aid learning in your family? Have some of the subjects computers can help you learn caught your eye? Or can you envision the kids using the computer to do better in school? Perhaps it's a foreign language, a course on ancient history, a program on psychology, supervision skills in business, algebra, or chemistry. All these and many more are available for the ATARI Computers and there are more programs being added every month!

If you are thinking of a computer for your school or classroom, the features that make it a good "educational" computer will be the major considerations. On the other hand, if you are thinking of buying a computer for the home, educationally relevant features may be important but not paramount. Keep your application in mind as you read this chapter.

Although most of the personal computers available today can be used as learning aids, there are features which are more important in a learning environment than in other settings. Chapter 2 is a detailed guide to buying a personal computer. You should consider this chapter as a supplement to Chapter 2. It deals with the most important questions to ask before buying an educational computer for the school or home. If you haven't done so yet, please read Chapters 2 and 7.

In Chapter 2, we introduced seven buying steps that we feel you should follow. Steps 4, 5, 6 and 7 are exactly the same for an educational computer, so we won't repeat them.

There are, however, some special considerations that are unique to educational computers; therefore, we have expanded the first three steps.

STEP ONE. IDENTIFY USES

Will the computer be used in the home as an aid to elementary and high school students learning basic skills? Will parents use it in their educational program? Is it destined, instead, for a prominent place in the new office machines room at your high school? Perhaps it is being purchased for a junior college program on microcomputers, or a college course in microbiology. The intended uses will determine how you answer the questions in Step 2.

STEP TWO. SOFTWARE CONSIDERATIONS.
WHAT SOFTWARE IS AVAILABLE?

It goes without saying that you must have educational programs to have an educational computer. Lack of available programs, in fact, has been one of the major reasons why computers are not more common in classrooms. If you have a particular application in mind, be sure the computer you buy has programs for that application. If you plan to write your own programs, be sure to buy a computer that has an easy to use educational language such as PILOT or BASIC. One reason Atari has been able to move into the educational market quickly is the availability of many educational programs that run on the ATARI Computers. Part of the reason there are many educational programs for the ATARI Computers is the company's willingness to cooperate with and assist others who want to write programs for their computers. Many less popular computers, even those with very good designs, simply have not attracted the attention required to induce educational publishers and software writers to develop programs for them.

STEP THREE. SPECIFY MINIMUM REQUIREMENTS
AND PREFERRED KEY FEATURES

Is It Easy To Learn To Use?

Computers in schools are used by many different students and often by many different teachers as well. If there is too much *learning overhead,* that is, if the computer is so complicated to use that it takes each user five or ten hours to learn to turn the machine on, load a program and begin using it, the system is not suitable for educational applications.

Computers designed primarily for business applications often require a one-to-five day training program for primary operators. A business can afford such a time investment if there are only a few people who will use the computer, and there is not a high staff turnover rate. Since there is a new crop of students each semester or year, the educational computer must be relatively easy to learn to use.

Even if the computer will be used in the home for educational purposes its operation should be simple enough that younger children in the family can operate it independently.

Is The Computer Friendly?

Many people approach a computer with considerable trepidation and anxiety. Even if the computer is relatively easy to use the anxious operator who expects it to be difficult to use will find that it is. The design of the computer should be such that a new user feels relatively comfortable using it. An attractive case, simple but functional keyboard, use of color coding, and absence of any *doomsday* keys all contribute to a friendly computer. A *doomsday* key is a key that, when pressed by accident, will destroy the program in the computer's memory. There are few things worse for a first time computer user than being told *Whatever you do, don't hit this key; if you do it will destroy everything in memory!* The anxious learner often spends more time trying to stay away from that key than in learning to use the computer (and it is, of course, the first key the curious learner pushes).

The ATARI 800 Computer is a good example of what you should look for; protection from a doomsday key. It has a key labeled SYSTEM RESET. It is a handy key when you want to clear the screen and start over. It does not erase programs from memory; it simply erases them from the screen. When accidently pressed in the middle of some programs, however, its effect can be disconcerting. It is placed well away from the other keys, it is a different color, and it has a plastic guard around it. It is almost impossible to press it without intending to.

Computer programs can also have *doomsday* instructions in them. Some word processing programs have instructions that

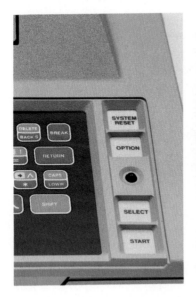

The ATARI 400 and 800 Computers are user friendly. Notice the clearly marked and protected SYSTEM RESET buttons.

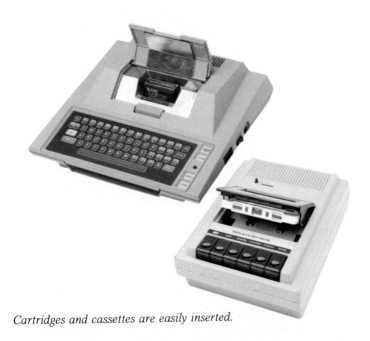

Cartridges and cassettes are easily inserted.

delete everything you have typed into the computer's memory. A student who has just spent six hours of hard work typing in a term paper will be understandably upset if he or she inadvertently hits a key that erases everything before it is printed. A *friendly* word processing program will make it difficult to erase large amounts of material (e.g. require pressing several keys at once rather than one or two). For example, the ATARI Word Processing program will ask ARE YOU SURE? before doing something drastic. You must respond yes, before anything happens.

What Kind Of Input Options Are Available?

Some computers only permit the user to talk to it through the keyboard. That is convenient for some purposes and inefficient for others. Educational programs can often take advantage of other input options such as joystick controllers.

Virtually any computer will display letters and numbers on the screen. At the other end of the continuum, some are capable of generating complicated sound output, special characters and very sophisticated color graphics as well as text. The interest and sophistication of educational programs are enhanced by sound and by good color graphics. It is one thing to read about how a nuclear reactor works; it is something entirely different to watch an animated model of a reactor appear on the screen and go through each of its cycles. Not only is this ATARI display more interesting than the text, it can actually teach many concepts far better than simple text.

It is generally accepted that the ATARI Computers have exceptional color graphics. ("The ATARI Home Computer System has vastly greater graphics capabilities than any other personal computer." Chris Crawford, *Compute*, January, 1981. "No home computer has the range of sophisticated graphic capabilities that the ATARI 400 and 800 Computers have. There are no STAR RAIDERS clones for the Apple or TRS-80 because those machines are simply unable to imitate the smooth player motion of the ATARI. They are also unable to quickly mix text and graphics the way the ATARI can." Paul Hoffman, *Creative Computing*, June, 1981. "I've been in computer graphics for twenty years and I lay awake night after night trying to understand how that ATARI machine did what it did. . . The ATARI machine is the most extraordinary computer graphics box ever made." Ted Nelson, *Creative Computing,* June, 1980.) An often overlooked feature of the ATARI Computers, however, is the dual track tape recorder. It has one track for recording the computer program and another track for audio. Several educational programs for ATARI Computers use the audio track to provide spoken instructions and explanations while displaying text and illustrations on the screen. Since the computer can control the tape recorder, it is possible, for example, to print a French word or phrase on the screen, and then let the student hear a correct pronunciation of it as well. In another application, the audio track can help young children use the computer even if they can't read and understand written instructions. The audio track has applications in many educational programs for providing directions, instructions, and test items. Look for a computer that has both audio and data tracks on its cassette system.

Is It Kid Proof?

No electronic equipment is completely immune from prying hands and inquisitive minds, but an educational computer should be designed so that a child cannot easily damage it or be damaged by it. Recently we saw an electronic cash register completely destroyed in a cafeteria when a customer accidently spilled a large cup of coffee onto the keyboard while reaching for change in his pocket. The cash register's keyboard was a standard *open* type with a circuit board located just under the keys. The coffee shorted out the machine and did so much damage the cash register had to be junked.

Many computers have keyboards with circuits just under them. They are more likely to be damaged by a liquid spilled on the keyboard than computers like the ATARI 400 Computer which use a *membrane* keyboard. Membrane keyboards are usually made of one piece of embossed plastic that does not allow anything to get between the keys and into the computer itself.

Some computers also present a significant hazard to children because high voltages are present at locations which are easy to get to. Several popular systems with removable tops or cases, for example, have a potentially *lethal* 120 volts at several unprotected locations. An educational computer should not be too easy to disassemble. If using the computer does require removal of part of the cover or case, access should not expose the user to *lethal* voltages. The ATARI Computers have a removable top that pops up to allow insertion of memory cartridges and program modules. As an extra safety feature, the ATARI Computers turn off when the top is lifted. The actual computer circuit board, however, can only be reached by turning the computer over and removing several screws in the bottom of the case.

Another aspect of kid proofing is the way accessories are connected to the computer. Connectors should be clearly labeled, and there should be little or no likelihood of connecting something to the wrong plug. Some computers, for example, use the same type of connector for the power cord and the accessories. Accidently plugging the power cord into the wrong socket can produce a variety of unwanted fireworks. ATARI Computer accessories plug in only one way, the right way and in only one place, the right place, thereby eliminating potential dangers.

To summarize, an educational computer should be safe and protected from accidents and likely human errors.

Is There A Special Pricing Arrangement?
What Kind Of Service Is Available?

Several computer manufacturers, recognizing the importance of educational computing, offer schools a special price break. Atari offers an *educational discount* to schools, as do several other manufacturers. Virtually all the major companies are involved in at least a few demonstration projects.

Service, which was discussed in detail in Chapter 3, is particularly important in an educational setting. Class meets whether the computer is working or not, thus dependability and service are important.

The remaining steps in buying an educational computer are the same as the general steps outlined in Chapter 2. Look at your budget, try the computers out, locate a suitable source, and buy it.

From the top to the bottom: joysticks, game paddles, THE EDUCATOR™ kit, ATARI 410™ Program Recorder and two educational programs.

The quality of graphics in educational simulation programs can enhance learning.→

SUMMARY

In addition to the general considerations discussed in Chapter 2, if you are going to buy an educational computer, you should pay particular attention to the following features:

1. Easy to learn to use.
2. User friendly – does not intimidate first time users; has no *doomsday* features.
3. Multiple input options – has provisions for accessories such as game paddles and joysticks.
4. Output options – color displays, graphics and sound are all desirable features.
5. Kid proofing – the computer should not present a danger to young and curious users, and it should not be easy to damage by accident or human error.
6. Programs – Are they available and are they both what you want and need?
7. Service and, if you are a school or college, special pricing arrangements. A broken computer can't teach. Check out service carefully.

Chapter 9

Solving Business and Professional Problems

How well you manage your three major resources: *time, talent and treasure,* will determine how successful you are. A computer should be used to optimize one or more of these resources. In this chapter we will show you how. We will discuss both kinds of working computers: the professional or managerial computer and the business computer. A business computer will help you manage your day to day business operations efficiently and economically. A professional computer will help you manage your time efficiently. A managerial computer can help provide you with better information for making business decisions by helping you answer the "what would happen if" questions. We will start with an introduction to managerial and professional applications of computers.

MANAGERIAL USES OF SMALL COMPUTERS

In the future, how well you use a computer may determine how successful you are. You are probably familiar with the old adage, "Genius is 90% perspiration and 10% inspiration." A computer can't do anything about the 10% but it sure can make the 90% a lot easier. No matter what your profession, you spend a large portion of your time doing humdrum chores. A computer can relieve you from the humdrum and give you more time to be a genius. Here are 15 things you can do with a small computer:

1. Write letters or proposals
2. Send a personalized letter to 10,000 prospects

3. Send a personalized collection letter to all overdue accounts
4. Bill clients
5. Prepare a budget
6. Analyze your cash flow
7. Do a sales forecast
8. Analyze program effectiveness; i.e., response to ads
9. Analyze and determine sales territories
10. Prepare cost/benefit ratios
11. Make pricing decisions
12. Do statistical analysis
13. Make purchasing decisions
14. Analyze cost effectiveness
15. Make purchasing projections

Because of the versatility of small computers, no one can describe all of their uses. We can, however, describe some of their functions in detail. Hopefully, you will then be able to assess small computers in terms of your own needs and interpolate how you will use one.

WORD PROCESSING

We will start with that boon to secretaries and writers – the word processor. If you write anything – letters, reports, articles, books – word processing can be a big time saver. For example, have you ever written a letter, had it typed, and then found something you wanted to change? With a typewriter, it usually means typing the entire letter over and reproofing everything. With a word processor, making a change is a minor adjustment and after you have made the change you can print out a letter perfect copy. Word processors let you store a copy of the letter on cassette or diskette and reuse it. Changes involve no more than loading the letter back into the computer's memory (from the diskette), making your changes, and printing another copy. The same procedure is used to revise and update reports, articles, and chapters of books. In fact, we wrote this book on an ATARI 800 Computer using word processing.

What is word processing? One expert defined it as "an automated system designed to cut the cost and time of some basic office routines – specifically the originate-dictate, check-type-retype cycle of producing business documents"

The ATARI Word Processor allows you to print out each page individually, or all pages in a document.

(from *Management's Guide to Word Processing* by Walter A. Kleinschrod published by Dartnell). Whatever you call it, it is an efficient way to produce written material that can save you enough money to pay for your computer in a year or less. Let's look at how you can do this. If you have a secretary who types 60 words a minute, she probably slows down to four or five words a minute when all the white-outs and retypings are taken into account. Word processing saves all this time. White-outs and retyping are not necessary. In addition, she can type a lot faster because there are no carriage returns except at the end of paragraphs. The computer determines the

line length with a unique feature called page formatting. If your secretary is word processing from dictation, she can probably output material five times as fast. If she spends about one-half of her time typing, and you pay her $900.00 a month with an allowance of 30% for benefits and overhead, you'll easily pay for your small computer in less than six months. This gives you an opportunity to make your secretary into a true assistant who can relieve you from some of your work. In most small businesses, relieving the boss of extra work is a good way to increase profits.

To give you an overview of word processing, we will describe a typical system. The ATARI Word Processor system includes: an ATARI 800 Computer with 48K of RAM, at least one ATARI 810 Disk Drive, an ATARI 850 Interface Module, an ATARI 825 80-Column Printer, and the word processing package. You are probably wondering what all these things are so we'll briefly describe each one.

The ATARI 800 Computer shown on page 101 is set up for word processing. It uses a standard television as a monitor, or if you prefer, it can be attached to a computer monitor (as monitors cost as much or more than a TV and can only be used with a computer, you are probably better off using a TV). It can store 30,000 characters (it actually has room to store 49,152 characters but the word processing program needs to be stored in memory also).

The ATARI 810 Disk Drive can store your data (information) permanently. Data is stored on a piece of plastic, about the size of a 45 rpm record, called a diskette. Each diskette will hold about 70 pages of text.

The ATARI 850 Interface Module connects the computer to both the printer and the disk drive at the same time.

The ATARI 825 80 column printer uses $8\frac{1}{2} \times 11$-inch paper. The paper can be fanfold (the sheets are attached to each other with perforated seams and removable sprocket holes in the sides), roll stock, or sheets (letterhead, for instance). The printer will print 85 to 132 characters (depending on whether you want pica or elite type) on each line, so the average business letter will fit nicely.

All of the equipment comes with the cables and manuals necessary to make hookup and operation easy. In fact, one of the things we find most impressive is the attention to the needs of first time computer users.

The ATARI Word Processor package consists of two diskettes, a cassette and two manuals. The actual word processing program is on the Program Master Diskette and there is a comprehensive reference manual that goes with it. An independent study course is also provided. The training program consists of an audio tape, a training data diskette, and a workbook. The workbook is divided into six lessons of increasing difficulty. The audio tape is used in the first two lessons and the information on the tape is repeated in the workbook. Like other ATARI products, the word processing is easy to learn and use.

The best way to use a word processor is to type in your document without worrying about mistakes. Then run off a printed copy (or hard copy), make your changes on the hard copy and type the changes into the computer. If you are doing this for yourself, you will probably want to skip the hard copy stage until you have made all of the corrections. In fact, one of the best ways to use a word processor in business is to type the information in yourself rather than dictating it or writing it out long hand. When you have finished, your secretary can make the necessary changes, prepare the envelope and run off the hard copy. It doesn't take you any extra time (in all probability it will take you less time) and it saves your secretary a lot of time.

Changes are quite easy. You can go to any part of the text at random. The computer sets up a *window* that shows a screen full of material. You can move this window left or right, up or down by characters, lines, paragraphs or pages. This feature is called scrolling. Using the *move* command you can move a block of text anywhere within the document and if you want, you can insert new material. You insert material by either typing it in or loading it in from a diskette. These features are common to most word processors but the ATARI Word Processor program has some that aren't common. Here they are:

Decimal Align – This is a special tab feature that allows you to enter columns of numbers that automatically line up by decimal point.

Sales

1. Are your sales projections accurate?
2. Are sales made to the same customers or are new customers constantly being added and old customers being dropped?
3. What are your terms?

General Overhead

1. What are your fixed expenses?
2. Is your payroll fixed or variable?
3. Can some of your fixed expenses be paid quarterly rather than monthly?

Banking

1. At what rate do you borrow money?
2. Can you increase revenue by using savings accounts?

Now let's look at a specific department of a business – marketing. Marketing is an enigma to almost everyone. No matter what business you are in, it is difficult to prove that marketing is effective. Consequently, everyone wants to cut the marketing budget. This means that marketing budgets are carefully scrutinized by management. To make matters worse, good marketing managers are usually not numbers oriented. The small computer gives a marketing manager (or any other manager for that matter) an opportunity to produce sensible budgets. Here are some of the factors that a marketing manager needs to consider:

Sales Forecasts

1. How accurate have the sales forecasts been in the past?
2. What is the product mix?
3. How many new products will you introduce this year?

Advertising

1. How much should you spend on space advertising?
2. Should you do direct mail?
3. How much do "free" promotions cost you?

Salary Expense

1. Are you charged a general overhead expense?
2. Do you need any additional staff?

All of these factors – and quite a few more – can be reduced to percentages. You probably do something like this now. If you are not using a computer, this probably takes you many hours and sometimes you are still off by quite a bit. With a computer, not only can you make more accurate forecasts, but you can also experiment with a wide variety of scenarios. Most managers like to think hypothetically, *What would happen if---*Your computer can give you this capability and it can give it to you in color. For instance, imagine using a bar graph to show cash flow. You could use black to show months in which cash flow is adequate, green for months when there is an excess and red for. . . well, you know what red means. As you change the factors involved, the graph would change accordingly.

One of the key elements of a cash flow projection is the sales forecast. The sales forecast is usually made by the sales manager or marketing manager. If you are a sales manager, your real interest is people, and not a bunch of numbers on a piece of paper. Most sales managers think of sales projections as absolute drudgery, but forecasts are part of the job, so you do them. Well, we have some good news and some bad news. The bad news is that you are still going to have to make out reports and do forecasts. The good news is that your computer will make it easier. Think about this: isn't most of what you project based on *educated guessing?* Obviously, a computer can handle numbers; all you have to do is tell it what numbers to handle and what to do with them.

Many managers already recognize that small computers are an invaluable tool, consequently, there are some very good programs available. VisiCalc* is one of the most popular and useful programs ever developed. It allows you to construct an electronic worksheet that replaces your pencil, paper and calculator. Your cash flow and many other problems can be

---

*VisiCalc is a trademark of VisiCorp, Inc.

analyzed using VisiCalc. The electronic worksheet is organized into a set of rows and columns that intersect at data points. At each point you can enter an alpha/numeric title, a number or a formula. You can then instruct the computer to format each entry by row and column.

It is difficult to describe VisiCalc so we suggest you have it demonstrated. However, let's look at an example. Assume that you want to prepare a cash flow analysis. You start by entering all of the data, i.e., sales, payroll, office expenses, etc. You then enter a simple formula that computes your cash flow. VisiCalc changes all variables anytime you change any variable. Before you have it demonstrated, lay out a problem you want solved. You'll see that it's worth buying a computer just to have VisiCalc.

Sample Output from VisiCalc

VisiCalc belongs to a special class of programs called data base management systems (DBMS). In the typical system you start by specifying the type and relationship of information to be processed. Specification is easy because you have to give the file a name and define the number of characters expected in each answer. You can then manipulate the data in a variety of ways. For example, you might use a DBMS to assign sales territories, or you might use it to figure out how much you make on every shoe you repair.

Perhaps you are not a manager, but you would like to be one. What can a computer do for you? First of all, you can use it for everything your manager does. Not only will you be able to produce better reports, but you will be gaining some valuable experience. If you are a sales representative you can keep your tickler file on your computer. (A tickler file is a list of customers, along with some pertinent information about each one). You can also keep a product file on your computer. A real estate agent for instance, might have a list of current prospects on one diskette and a list of houses on another diskette.

Small computers are not limited to strict business applications. Many professionals also use them.

If you are an attorney, you can bill your clients on a real time basis. Say you charge $50 an hour. If you spend one hour with Mr. Jones and one hour with Ms. Smith, do you charge them both the same amount? Suppose the Jones case requires three hours of legal assistant time and the Smith case requires only secretarial time. What do you do then? With a small computer you analyze each case individually and charge accordingly.

We could describe an almost endless variety of professions and show you how a computer increases productivity in each. We won't do that. We will say, however, that regardless of your profession, there is probably some way you can use a computer to improve the quality of your work and free up more of your time. There are even some ways you can tie into some other people's data bases and use their ideas and information. These applications are explained in Chapter 5, THE OUTER LIMITS.

We hope you will use your computer to stave off recession, whip inflation, progress in your business, enhance your profession, write books, analyze investments or make yourself rich. Whatever your applications are, we know you will find it useful.

SMALL BUSINESS COMPUTERS

If you are in business, you need a computer. It is as simple as that. You may think that your business is too small, but if it supports you, then it is not too small to benefit from a computer. Every company, from the giant corporation to the neighborhood service station or local real estate office, can use a computer. You already know about giant corporate computers, so let's talk about a service station owner. Let's call him Joe.

The Down Home Gas and Supply, as Joe calls his station, is a popular place. Joe sells gas at 10 cents above his cost and he charges only $15.00 an hour for mechanical work. Best of all, he is an excellent mechanic. His profits from his gas sales cover most of his overhead, but he does have to do some mechanical work to break even. Therefore, his earnings come from his mechanical work and the sale of parts. When he adds parts and labor together, his gross profit on mechanical work is about $17.00 an hour. He spends about 30 hours a month on his books (1 hour a night and 4 to 5 hours extra at month's end). This is 30 hours he could spend doing mechanical work. If he can cut the bookwork down to 10 hours a month, he will increase his monthly revenue by $340.00. He can do this with a computer that costs less than $175.00 a month, assuming that he buys a computer that costs about $5000.00 and pays for it over a three-year period. At the end of three years, he will own the computer and his expenses will be limited to maintenance.

A computer won't solve all of Joe's problems, but it will help. Not only will it increase his profits by allowing him more time to do mechanical work, it will also help in other areas. For instance, using careful inventory control, he can be sure he has enough of the parts he needs and he can return or sell those he doesn't need. This feature alone could save him enough money to pay for the computer.

Small computers are so inexpensive that any business can afford one. Most small computer manufacturers have an accounting package that will meet Joe's needs. As recently as 1975, a computer with these capabilities would have cost upwards of $50,000 and the programs needed for accounting purposes could easily have doubled the cost.

The real key to buying a business computer is determining how you are going to use it. To do this you need to make a careful survey of your business. You should know how you are going to use your computer and why. Start your survey by analyzing how you sell your product (or service). There are some basic questions you should ask yourself about your business. These questions are:

Accounts Receivable and Cash

1. How many of your customers pay cash?
2. What is the age of your averge A/R?
3. What is your bad debt ratio?
4. How do you check credit?

If you can efficiently control your accounts receivables, you should be able to control cash flow.

Accounts Payable

1. What are your average accounts payable by day? Week? Month?
2. Do you use purchase orders?
3. Do you take advantage of fast payment discounts?
4. What is the length of time from placing a purchase order to the time of delivery?
5. How are disbursements made?
6. What reports do you require?

This is an area where a computer can pay for itself in a real hurry. Many small businesses don't bother with purchase orders because *they take too much time,* consequently, they miss discounts due to inattention.

Payroll

1. How many employees do you have?
2. What is the average employee turnover time?
3. Are your employees salaried or hourly or both?
4. Do you offer overtime, vacation or sick pay?
5. How do you handle federal, state and local withholding taxes?
6. What reports do you require?

Payroll checks and reports require an enormous amount of repetitive work. A computer can perform this chore quickly, efficiently and accurately.

If your business is product oriented you will also want to consider these factors:

Inventory

1. What are your product categories?
2. Are your products packaged individually?
3. Are there pricing considerations for quantity?
4. How many new items are added or deleted per month?
5. How many finished products are in inventory?
6. How do you keep track of cost and minimum/maximum levels?
7. What reports are required?

In short, how do you control inventory and how can a computer help you control it better?

Order Entry

1. What is your average number of orders per day?
2. What is the highest number you expect to ever enter per day?
3. Do you have any *bill to/ship to* customers?
4. How many line items per order?
5. How many types of customers do you service?
6. How are back orders processed?
7. What reports are required?

After you have done a complete analysis of your business, then you can define the specific jobs you expect your computer to perform. Because the computer is merely a tool, it must have a specific job. If you define these jobs carefully, your selection process will be a lot easier. There are five key questions you need to ask yourself. These questions are:

1. What data must I get from the computer?
2. What form should this data be in?
3. How much storage do I need?
4. What is it going to take to input my data?
5. What would I like the computer to accomplish?

We will define the term data here, but you don't have to understand the term to understand this process. Data are the

An ATARI 800 Computer determines costs in a shoe repair shop.   ➞

facts and figures you use in your business. Starting with item one above, the first thing to do is make a list of the data you want from your computer. A sample list for Joe's service station is shown below:

1. Gas pumped on a daily, weekly, monthly and yearly basis.
2. Customer list including home address, phone number and type of car (or cars) and perhaps a maintenance record for each.
3. Inventory of parts carried, including what is selling and what isn't. For instance, do we sell more radial tires than two-plys, and what is the difference in profit margin on these items?
4. Bookkeeping: keeping track of payroll, taxes, sales, etc. Maybe we can come up with some reports that will save the accountant some time.

Once you've made your list, revise it. If someone else is interested in your business, ask for help. Try to think of every possible use for your computer, and don't overlook the *soft* uses, such as using your computer as a promotional aid. There are a lot of things that you don't do now because you don't have time. Can any of these things be done by a computer?

The four remaining questions should be fairly easy to answer once you've answered Question One carefully. Information or data is of little use to you if you have to spend a great deal of time interpreting it. Do you need word descriptions of items or will numbers do? What form do you want this data to be in? What form do you have it in now and how can you improve it?

Data storage capacity can be expensive. A moderate increase in your storage requirements can, in some cases, increase the cost of your system by as much as 50% or more. The little 5¼-inch diskette systems can store 100K+ on a single diskette. The 8-inch systems store more but cost a lot more, and the hard disk systems that store millions of items of data are big buck systems. Therefore, take care in answering Question Three. Break your needs down into two categories, short term and long term. Short term should mean only data referred to and used daily. You'll be surprised at how little this really is. You should look at computers that can handle about double your short term load. You don't want to run out of memory right in the middle of order processing, but you don't want to buy more than you need. As a general rule, one 8½ × 11-inch double spaced, typewritten page requires a little less than 2K of memory for storage. Many small business needs can be met with 48K and one or two 5¼-inch disk drives. The 48K will hold less than 24 pages of data, since you'll have to have some memory space for the computer program itself. In reality you can probably get by with 32K, but memory is so inexpensive you might as well get the maximum available, which is usually 48K.

Question Four is a matter of form. Just as you have some preferred ways of getting data out, you probably have a preferred method of putting it in. If you answered the first three questions carefully, you know the answer to Question Four. One of the three primary resources is time. Don't waste time by using a computer that has a complicated input procedure.

A computer can help you get the most from your three resources, but you have to determine how. This is the purpose of Question Five. Make three lists with these headings: time, talent, treasure. Under each one, jot down ways you can optimize the use of these resources. For instance, under *treasure,* think about how you can manage your cash flow better. You might list all of your clerical and managerial needs under *talent* and analyze each. Are you making the most effective use of your employees? Most managers are real experts at operating machines; can you say the same thing about the people who work for you?

WHERE TO GO FROM HERE

If it sounds like you need an ATARI 800 Computer to help you figure all of this out, then you've discovered at least one managerial use for a computer. But, you do need to analyze these things even if you don't have a computer. Here is a plan that will probably work for you:

1. Get out a pencil and paper. Take a pass at answering the five key questions and at answering the other questions posed in this chapter.
2. Read the rest of this book and fill out the checklist in the back. (It's been good so far, hasn't it?)
3. Read some other books and some magazine articles on

the subject. You'll find a list of magazine and book publishers in Chapter 14.

4. Decide how much you can afford to spend.
5. Talk to several different vendors and look at lots of computers.
6. Before buying anything, read some more if possible.
7. Develop an awareness of what will really be required to implement a system in your business. Be prepared to spend enough time to determine all of your needs.

Buying a computer is a major undertaking regardless of the price of the computer. You will get the most out of your computer if you carefully analyze your situation and buy a system that fits both your current needs and expected future needs.

Chapter 10

Investing In A Computer For Your Business

When you buy a computer for your business, you are making a major decision. Therefore, you should be as careful as possible. If you haven't done so yet, we suggest that you read Chapters 2 and 9 before starting this one. In Chapter 2 we introduced a set of general buying guidelines. These steps are the same whether you are buying a small business computer or a managerial computer. Chapter 9 introduced you to the idea of using a computer in your business or profession. This chapter will show you how to fit a computer to your needs.

BUYING STEPS

Step One. Identify Your Major Uses

If you buy a typewriter or a truck, you have a specific use in mind. The same should be true when you buy a computer.

If you have followed the steps we outlined in Chapter 9, you should have a solid handle on how your business operates. Now, you need to pick out the single most important item that you want to computerize. If you are using the computer strictly for managerial applications, is the major use for your computer going to be word processing, cash flow analysis, sales analysis or something else? If you buy a computer, what is the single most important use for it? If you operate a small business, is your single most important use managerial applications or is it accounting?

Step Two. Determine Your Software Needs

There are several ways to acquire the software you will need. A specific computer manufacturer may have developed software that is ideal for your use. For instance, if you have a managerial application, you will want to buy the ATARI Word Processor and VisiCalc. Both programs are excellent manufacturer supplied software.

Your next option is to go to a systems house or a programmer and have the programs you need written for you. If you have done a careful analysis of your business, you may be able to keep costs in line. Your local computer dealer may be able to suggest someone. But, please bear in mind that this can be a very expensive process. There are a lot of canned programs already available, so be sure that what you want is not available before you hire someone to develop it for you.

Last, but certainly not least, you can develop or write the necessary software yourself. Programming is not that difficult to learn. For most applications, it is not as difficult to learn as something like bridge or chess, especially if you use a simple language like ATARI BASIC or ATARI PILOT.

All of these approaches work and you will probably want to use more than one. As for the last option, it will probably suit your interests and convenience some day to learn something about programming. Some day you will begin to wonder "Hm. I wonder if that thing will. . .?"

Step Three. Specify Minimum Requirements and Preferred Features

This is where you get down to the real nitty-gritty. The hardware items you want for sure are a computer with 48K of memory, a disk drive and a good printer. There are exceptions to this rule though. If you use your computer in a dusty or dirty environment, you will probably want to get a small membrane keyboard computer. An ATARI 400 Computer, for instance, may be ideal for some manufacturing applications. The minimum software packages you want are a financial modeling package or a data base manager and a word processing package. But what else do you need? If you are going to use your computer in your small business, you will need an accounting package, but what size? Is your business service oriented or product oriented? If it is product oriented, you will need an inventory package. If it is service oriented, you may want a package that is specifically adapted to your needs, i.e. a real estate package.

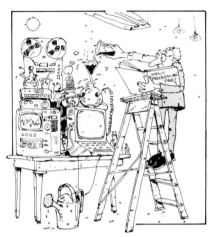

Step Four. Identify Likely Secondary Uses and Desirable Machine Features

For instance, you will certainly want to use your computer as a managerial aid. There are some managerial applications that can be greatly enhanced by color but you might not see any use for color in your primary application. You might also want to consider using your computer as a training tool. As an example, you might buy an inexpensive computer that has a limited accounting package on it and use it to teach key employees the rudiments of accounting. Some accounting packages have excellent training programs developed by well-recognized accounting firms. As another example, you might use your computer as a product orientation instructor for new employees, especially salespeople. As you can see, these applications are viable for not only small companies but also giant corporations.

Step Five. Decide How Much You Want to Spend— Now and Later

Are there ways of buying the computer that will save you money? Should you buy outright? Should you rent or lease? If

you do buy outright, should you pay cash or should you finance?

If you decide to lease, there are a variety of options available. If you get a standard lease, you will have the option of paying for your computer over a 36 month period (in fact, some leasing companies will give you up to 48 months). At the end of the leasing period you will most likely be able to buy the computer for 10% of the original purchase price.

Step Six. Have Computers Demonstrated

Once you decide to buy a computer, you can begin to evaluate different systems. To get the best results, you'll probably want to combine steps six and seven.

The best way to buy a small system is to "surround and outnumber 'em." In other words, take someone with you. If you are a manager or professional, take your assistant (or secretary). If you operate a small business, take your accountant. If possible, take two or three people with you. There are several reasons for doing this, but the two most important are distraction and fear. If you buy a computer, someone you know is going to feel threatened by it. If they get an opportunity to play with the computer, they won't be afraid of it. (In fact, if you really want to calm their fears, give them a copy of this book to read). When you go to the computer store, take someone along to distract the salespeople. Then, when you've got the computer to yourself – make it quit working. No, we don't mean take the fire ax to it. What you should do though is see what you can do to make the program stop. Just push buttons until everything goes wild. This is the best test of user friendliness we know. Once the computer starts doing wild things, have someone show you how to make it work properly again. If the procedure is simple and clear cut, the computer is friendly. But, beware of salesmen who say, "Oh, that's easy to fix" and don't show you how to solve the problem. Have them show *you* how to solve the problem. If possible, get them to show you how to look it up in the documentation.

Step Seven. Buy It

It is probably best to go to an established dealer, but it is not crucial. It depends on your definition of *established dealer.*

← *A small computer is a time-saving office tool and managerial aid.*

Most of the dealers were not even in business five years ago, so judge all of them essentially the same. Find out as much as you can about the people who own and run the store. Try to find someone who has a real interest in computers, in business applications and in your business.

POTENTIALLY IMPORTANT FEATURES

In this section, we describe the features you will need for a managerial computer. If all you want is a business computer, you won't need some of these features. However, we would suggest that you consider them anyway. After all, a business owner is first and foremost a manager. The minimum system you will need is:

Display:	24 × 40 Characters
Keyboard:	Full-sized typewriter-style
Storage medium:	Disk drive
Main memory:	48K (RAM)
Printer:	Letter quality

We have talked about these features in other chapters, so we will only briefly review them here. A 40 character line is about all anyone can read at a single glance so it is adequate for most business uses. A display that uses a longer line usually costs quite a bit more. A shorter length line can be quite frustrating. If you occasionally use words that are longer than 10 characters (such as occasionally) you might wind up with vertical sentences. Good computer systems use a feature called *wrap-around* that drops words to the next line when they won't fit. This is also an important feature. One last comment about displays, be sure that the computer will display both upper case and *lower case letters.*

You should have a full-size typewriter-style keyboard. A numeric keypad is also nice but not necessary for many managerial applications. The keyboard should have a nice solid feel to it and no keybounce.

Although you can buy a cassette-based system for your computer, you don't want it. It's too slow for most business applications. The only acceptable storage medium for business applications is disk. You might be able to get by with a single disk drive but we would suggest that you have at least two.

Your main memory should be 48K. This means that you have room for a program, the operating system (the program that operates the computer) and probably 15 or so double spaced 8½ × 11-inch typewritten sheets.

A letter quality printer is a must for outside communications but many of your internal needs can probably be served with a less expensive thermal printer. You will have to determine what you mean by a letter quality printer. Many people believe that this means it has to look like a typewriter or slightly better. We're not sure. You can probably fill a lot of your needs with a dot matrix printer. We printed out all the drafts of this book on a dot matrix printer, the ATARI 825 80-Column Printer. We found that the type style is easier to read than most other letter quality typefaces, such as typewriters.

Be sure to price your computer system as a whole rather than looking at individual parts. The best thing to do is to explain to your dealer exactly what you want, what you are going to do with it and why. Then have the dealer work you up a price based on your needs.

Chapter 11

The Stuff That Makes It Happen: Software

For the beginner, computers often appear just short of magical. Even with their covers off, computers give few hints of how they operate. There are no gears turning, no dials revealing tell-tale signs of activity.

The working components of small computers are integrated circuits (ICs) which have no moving parts. In fact, most of an IC is just protective plastic. Sealed inside all that plastic is a tiny silicon chip which does all the work. The silicon chip is so small it can be placed on the tip of your finger with room left for several thousand angels (at least) to dance around, too.

If computer machinery seems mysterious, computer software (the programs or instructions the computer follows) is equally amazing. If the computer were a kitchen, the software would be a recipe to be followed. Just as there are many different types of recipes, so too are there many different types of software. In this chapter we will deal with two aspects of software. We will start with a brief introduction to the languages computers use. As computer languages are presented we will also deal with the types of computer software or programs written in those languages.

We don't want you to get the impression that you *must* learn to program a computer to be able to use it. It is nice to be able to write some of your own programs, or to at least know enough to modify and adapt the programs written by others. It really isn't necessary, though. (How many of us really know how our stereo works?) With the boom in small computers that has occurred over the last five years, there are thousands of programs just sitting on dealers' shelves or waiting in the computer magazines.

We have said it several times already but it bears repeating. You don't have to master computer programming to use a small computer. There are plenty of *canned* programs out there that run on your computer. Just like recorded music, all you have to do is plug in a cartridge or load a program into the computer's memory from a cassette or disk. Jerry's ten-year-old daughter, Amy, uses her computer regularly with all sorts of educational programs and games. Although Amy uses her computer often, she has not yet mastered BASIC, the most common computer language today. All she has to do to run her favorite programs is insert a cartridge or tell the computer to load a program from the tape recorder. When the computer tells her it is ready, Amy can press the START key or type RUN and begin playing her game. Maybe later she will tackle BASIC or PILOT. For now, she's convinced computers are neat, fun machines.

LANGUAGES FOR COMPUTERS

The computer in your home or business probably speaks several languages. No, it won't converse fluently in French or Spanish, but it will probably speak BASIC, maybe Pascal or PILOT, and probably some dialect of a cryptic group of languages called *machine language.*

The particular central processing unit (CPU) chip used in a computer determines which *machine language* it speaks. A CPU chip, often also called a microprocessor chip, is the

heart of a small computer. The ATARI Computers, for example, use a 6502 CPU chip. Not unexpectedly, the ATARI Computers speak 6502 machine language. (They also have a unique specialized chip that produces the spectacular ATARI graphics).

Although much of the software in a computer is written in machine language, most beginners will want to leave that language to experienced programmers. It is hard to use, very tedious, and time-consuming for the programmer. To use it requires some dedicated study of the machine language used in your system. Machine languages also use funny number systems (hexidecimal, octal, or – heaven forbid – binary) instead of the familiar family favorite, decimal. Here is an excerpt from a machine language program:

Column

1	2	3
004000	072	LDA
004001	037	
004002	006	
004003	117	MOV C,A

All the numbers are written in octal, a base-8 number system. The first column of numbers (004000) specifies the memory cell in the computer where the instruction is to be placed. The second column (072) lists the actual instructions. Computers don't understand words or letters, so everything must be converted to numbers before the CPU chip can actually process the information. The 072 in the first line of this excerpt will cause the computer to perform a particular function. In this case it takes the two numbers that immediately follow the instruction (037 and 006 in this program) and puts them in a special storage location inside the CPU chip. The last column lists a sort of shorthand summary of what the computer will do as the instructions are executed. The term LDA, for example, stands for *Load the Accumulator with the contents of the memory location selected by the numbers that follow.* MOV C,A means *Move whatever is in storage location A to storage location C.* The computer only deals with the numbers in the second column, the machine language instructions. (The first column tells the user where to put the instructions in the computer's memory and the third column is helpful when you want to read the listing of a machine language program and figure out what's happening.)

It takes thousands of the machine language instructions to perform even a simple job like keeping track of a list of names that will be printed on mailing labels. Again, we would suggest that you wade into machine language programming only after you've gained a lot of experience with an easier language like ATARI BASIC.

In between BASIC and machine language is something called *assembly language.* Remember LDA and MOV C,A in the previous excerpt? Using a special program called an Assembler, it is possible to type in phrases like LDA and MOV C,A and have them automatically converted into the proper machine language codes by the computer. The ATARI Assembler Editor cartridge helps you write, edit and run machine language programs on the ATARI Computers. It is one of several assembler programs available for the ATARI Computers. Since it is much easier to remember what MOV C,A means than it is to remember numbers like 117, assembly language work is a lot easier than machine language. It is still necessary to know the intimate details of machine language programming, however, before assembly language work can be done. Take heart though, there is another way.

Higher-level languages allow a beginner to start working with the computer in a very short period of time. This family of languages uses English-like words and mostly decimal numbers in the programming process. The best known of these languages, BASIC, is easy to learn. A weekend's work with a good BASIC instruction manual is enough to get a person started nicely. BASIC stands for Beginners All-Purpose Symbolic Instruction Code. Here is an example of ATARI BASIC:

```
10 DIM N$(25)
20 PRINT "HELLO, WHAT IS YOUR NAME?"
30 INPUT N$
40 PRINT "WELL, ";N$;" I'M GLAD YOU'VE COME
   OVER. I WAS LONELY."
```

THE PROGRAMMER™ kit, a simple way to learn BASIC.   ⟶

THE
PROGRAMMER™

ATARI 400 COMPUTER SYSTEM

BASIC

ATARI 400/800™
BASIC
REFERENCE
MANUAL

ATARI 400/800™

COMPUTING LANGUAGE
BASIC

CONTAINS ONE CARTRIDGE CXL 4002
USE WITH ATARI 400/800™ COMPUTER SYSTEMS

BASIC

ATARI 400

ATARI 800

As you can see, BASIC is more familiar than machine or assembly language. In BASIC each line of instructions has a line number. The line number tells the computer which instruction it is supposed to execute first, second, etc. The four lines shown here are numbered in increments of 10. They could have been numbered 1, 2, 3 and 4 or 49, 61,168 and 333. The computer doesn't care. It is best to always leave plenty of room between lines just in case you need to go back and add extra lines to the program. Between line 10 and line 20 in this program at least nine more lines could be added (e.g. 11, 12, 13, and so on). The computer starts with the lowest number.

BASIC understands a set of keywords which have a specific meaning for the computer. In the example the keywords PRINT and INPUT were used. Another keyword in BASIC is RUN. If you typed the four-line program into your computer and then typed RUN, the computer would begin executing the program. That is, it would look for the line with the smallest number (in this case line 10) and follow the instructions given there. Line 10 tells the computer that you can enter a name of up to 25 characters. Line 20 tells the computer to print the material between the quotation marks on the screen. Thus:

HELLO, WHAT IS YOUR NAME?

would appear on the screen. The keyword in line 20 is INPUT. It tells the computer to stop and wait for you to type in something on the keyboard. Suppose you type in CHARLIE. The computer takes CHARLIE and assigns it to the label N$. Now N$ equals CHARLIE. In line 30 the computer finds another PRINT instruction. It will print the following on the screen:

WELL, CHARLIE, I'M GLAD YOU CAME OVER. I WAS
    LONELY.

The computer printed everything inside the quotation marks just as it appeared (e.g. "WELL" and "I'M GLAD YOU CAME OVER. I WAS LONELY."). The N$ is not enclosed in quotation marks, however. Instead of printing out N$, the computer looked at its list of labels and found that N$ stands for CHARLIE. Thus it printed CHARLIE instead of N$.

BASIC is, without question, the most popular small-computer language today. It is used for a wide variety of applications from games to business to science and so on. More people work with BASIC than with FORTRAN or COBOL or any other language. There are, however, at least a hundred other high-level languages, each with a group of supporters who believe their language is the best. Some of the other languages are specialized. PILOT, for example, is designed expressly for dialog types of applications (you talk, computer replies, you respond, etc.) and is widely used in education. Others are general-purpose languages which were written because someone saw deficiencies in the currently available languages. Some people feel PILOT will soon replace BASIC as *the* beginner's language because it is easy to use yet powerful.

We do not want to leave you with the impression that BASIC is a single language and that BASIC on an ATARI Computer is the same as BASIC on a TRS-80 or an Apple II. BASIC is actually a family of languages. While it is relatively easy to shift from one version to another, there are real differences among the different versions of BASIC. ATARI BASIC, for example, has some very powerful instructions for creating color graphics and for producing computer generated sounds and music. Drawing a line on the screen with ATARI BASIC, for example, can be as simple as using the PLOT instruction to tell the computer where to start the line and using the DRAWTO instruction to tell it where the line should end. Some companies offer more than one version of BASIC. For example, you can get either ATARI BASIC or MICROSOFT* BASIC for an ATARI Computer.

COMPUTER SOFTWARE

When you shop for programs for your computer, the language they are written in is not likely to make all that much difference. The important thing will be – do they run on your computer and do what you want them to do? As long as that question is answered affirmatively, the language will be of little consequence to most people. Many game programs for ATARI Computers are written in machine language, but if

*Microsoft BASIC is a trademark of MicroSoft Inc., Bellevue, WA.

what you want to do is blast alien starships, you won't care. There are quite a few, however, which were written in BASIC. To be sure, there are differences in the way programs written in different languages operate. Machine language programs can do things much faster than BASIC programs. On the other hand, it will be easier for you to learn enough BASIC to modify and personalize a program written in BASIC. Many people like to tinker with programs they buy.

In any case there are hundreds, perhaps thousands, of programs available for small computers today. If you don't find what you're looking for at your local computer stores, Chapter 14 will tell you about other sources of information and programs.

If you would like to learn how to program in BASIC, there are over 100 books available and there are a large variety of books available on other languages. For instance, one of the best BASIC books we know of is *Instant [Freeze Dried Computer Programming in] BASIC, 2nd Astounding Edition.* In addition, you will want to carefully consider the ATARI Programmer kit. This ATARI kit is a self-teaching course in BASIC.

Chapter 12

It's Not Magic: The Basic Computer™

When we first became interested in computers, we read everything we could on the way computers work. We learned about computer memories, the signals that go out on parallel ports, handshaking, UARTS, RAM, ROM, integrated circuits, system clocks, data registers, and much, much more. This interest in the nuts and bolts of computers is reflected in Jerry's book, *Peanut Butter and Jelly Guide to Computers.* The plain fact of the matter, however, is that you don't really have to know anything about what goes on inside a computer to use it, just as you don't have to know a lot about video tape machines, automobiles or microwave ovens to use them.

Even though it is not really required, it might be nice to know how to build your own accessories for the computer and how to troubleshoot problems when they occur. But gaining that much knowledge takes a great deal of time and effort – effort which might be better invested in something else, such as learning how to program the computer. Then you would be able to write or customize your own programs. Our advice is to learn enough about the nuts and bolts of computers to carry on idle conversation at a party. Then concentrate on learning programming, if you really want to get into computers. Finally, after you've become proficient at programming in a computer language or two, go back to the hardware and dig a little deeper. For most people, developing programming skills pays off quicker. There is so much that can be done, and even a little knowledge of a popular language like BASIC can be of great benefit. Many people, in fact, will probably never get too involved in hardware. They will, instead, invest learning time in sharpening their programming expertise. This makes a great deal of sense. Technological advances in computer hardware can make much of what you've learned obsolete in a very short time. This is less likely to happen to a person who has learned to program a computer. Programming or software knowledge is also more portable than hardware knowledge. If you learn to program your computer in BASIC and PILOT, it won't be too difficult to switch to an improved model or to a new system which also uses BASIC or PILOT.

The remainder of this chapter presents a brief overview of a typical computer system. If this introduction to hardware only whets your appetite, the dilithium Press catalog contains a number of books which concentrate on computer hardware.

A SIMPLE COMPUTER SYSTEM

A typical, entry-level computer system is shown on page 120. While the printer may be a bit of an extravagance for the beginner, it is an absolute necessity for anyone who plans to use the computer for word processing or business applications. Computer systems from several manufacturers include all of the components shown on page 120, except the printer. In some cases the video monitor and disk drives are *optional* accessories. However, since you must have a monitor and a disk drive or tape recorder to use the computer, they really aren't optional – they just cost extra. Let's take a look at each of the components that make up a small computer system.

Power Supply

Not long ago power supplies for small computers were heavy brutes, designed to feed carefully filtered electrical energy to power-hungry circuits. Memory chips had particularly voracious appetites in the early microcomputers. Today, memory technology has progressed to the point where small computers require very little power. This has allowed designers to build smaller, less expensive power supplies which do a good job. The power supply alone in the old Sol 20 computer, for example, weighed more than three entire ATARI Home Computers.

Most computers require at least two voltages, +5 and +12. The power supply takes 115 volts AC (alternating current) from your wall plug and converts it to the DC (direct current) voltages required by the computer.

The power supply filters the line voltage so that a circuit requiring +5 volts gets +5 volts, no more and no less. Power supplies which lack adequate filtering tend to have *ripple* in their output. This means the voltage sent to the computer will average +5 volts but may actually waiver or ripple above and below 5 volts. Ripple can cause major problems in a computer. Fluctuations in the power supply voltage cause the system to malfunction or behave in an erratic manner.

Most of the current crop of computers have adequate power supplies. The ATARI 400 and ATARI 800 Computers, like many others, have a simple power supply designed to provide power only for the computer itself. Each additional accessory is supplied with its own power supply.

One more point should be made about power supplies. A large number of problems associated with the use of small computers in homes and businesses are due to line voltage fluctuations. Suppose, for example, that you have a very large central air conditioning unit on the same circuit as your computer. The computer may work flawlessly in the winter and then may work poorly or not at all in the summer. Line voltage may drop considerably when a heavy demand is placed on it. This phenomenon has become commonplace in many parts of the country and is known as *brownout*. Few computer power supplies are designed to deal with extreme fluctuations in line voltages. There are, however, a number of companies that sell special transformers which maintain constant voltage. Though expensive, they may be the only way to obtain dependable operation from a computer in some environments.

A related problem that can drive a computer user up the wall is a power line *glitch*. A glitch is a very brief spike of high voltage. Although the typical wall plug will provide around 115 volts, there are circumstances which may, for a fraction of a second, produce several thousand volts on the line. The erratic operation of one of our computers was finally traced to a large motor which was used to move air in a chilled water air conditioning system. Each time the motor turned on, it

caused the line voltage to drop slightly. It turned out that the power supply in our computer could handle that. When the motor turned off, however, it created a collapsing electrical field which fed a high voltage spike, or glitch, back into the electrical wiring of the building. Since it lasted only a split second, the most anyone noticed was a bit of static on the radio. But even that brief instant of high voltage was anathema to the computer. The spike rode into the power supply on the power line and was fed into the computer where it managed to royally confuse things. Programs that were working perfectly suddenly ran amuck. An automotive parts supply company whose computer was on the same power line as a welding shop experienced similar problems whenever the electrical welders were in use. Again, most computer power supplies are not designed to handle such a problem, but there are several inexpensive power line isolators and filters on the market that often cure *glitchitis* immediately.

Memory

Computers need quite a bit of memory or storage capability. All the instructions a computer follows, for example, must be stored somewhere in memory. Data to be analyzed is also usually stored in the computer's memory.

←*The ATARI BASIC cartridge is inserted in the top of the computer.*

Inside an ATARI 800 Computer. The 10K Operating System ROM and 48K of RAM are shown.

A computer's memory works much like a human memory. Information which will be used later is stored as electrical charges in memory *cells*. These are actually tiny sections of silicon that can be charged by an electrical impulse. The memory of most small computers is organized into *eight-bit bytes*. A bit is simply a place where a single piece of data is stored. A computer can store one *bit* in each memory cell. A bit can be either a 1 (*on*) or a 0 (*off*). Generally a cell that has an electrical charge in it is considered to be holding a *1*, while a cell with no charge in it is *0*.

By themselves the lowly bits can't do much. To make them more useful they are combined into *bytes*. This is a bit: 0, and this is a byte: 00110011. A byte is simply a set of eight bits. There are only two possible patterns for a bit: 1 and 0, but there are 256 possible patterns for a byte. Computers are programmed to treat each pattern as a code which can stand for a letter, number, or instruction. Computers can't deal directly with the letter A, but they can deal with a byte (a pattern of eight bits) which stands for A. The most commonly used code today is ASCII or American Standard Code for Information Interchange. The ASCII code for A is 01000001. Every upper and lower case letter, the numbers from 0 to 9, the most commonly used punctuation marks, and numerous computer control codes all have their own unique eight-bit code in ASCII.

Since the computer must deal with *eight-bit bytes* of data, the computer's memory is also organized into eight-bit bytes. If someone says their computer has *8K of memory* that translates into 8192 bytes of memory. The term K is an abbreviation for 1024. Thus 8K equals 8 × 1024 or 8192. Each byte of memory can hold the code for one letter or number. Since a typical, double-spaced, typewritten page will have less than 2000 characters on it, 8K of memory will hold at least four full pages. That really isn't much, which explains why many computers used for word processing generally have at least 32K of memory, enough to hold over 16 pages.

There are two major types of memory, ROM and RAM. ROM stands for *read only memory*. This kind of memory is generally programmed at the factory. The contents of ROM cannot be changed by the user. The ATARI Computers have a large cartridge of ROM memory that contains the *operating system software* for the computer. In essence, operating system software is a set of instructions that tells the computer what to do when the user gives the computer a direction. As you may have guessed, the game cartridge in video games also contains ROM. Each of the small program cartridges for ATARI Computers also contains ROM or pre-programmed memory.

To clarify the point, we should note that if we took the case of the ROM cartridges off, what we would find is a small circuit board with several integrated circuits on it. Most of the integrated circuits (ICs for short) would be ROM chips. By packaging most of the ROM for their computer in removable cartridges, Atari has made it easier to use the computer for many different jobs. Some computer manufacturers put the ROM that contains BASIC on the main computer board. It cannot be removed and thus takes up room in the computer's *memory map* whether it is being used or not. Most small computers can only accept a little over 64,000 bytes of memory. If a ROM with BASIC in it takes up 16,000 bytes of memory space all the time that means there is only 48K of memory available for other uses. Unless a computer is to be used for only one purpose it is better to have most or all the ROM in removable cartridges rather than permanently installed.

All computer memory cannot be ROM, however. Much of the memory in a computer is *random access memory* or RAM. The average home computer will contain 16K of RAM while a business computer system often has 48K or more of RAM, in addition to some ROM. RAM is also known as *volatile* memory and is general-purpose memory. You can store data or instructions in RAM, tell the computer to use the information you've stored, and then replace the material with something new. The biggest problem with RAM is that whatever is in it disappears when the computer is turned off. If you need to save something in RAM for use later, you must store it on tape or on disk before the computer is shut down. (Material in ROM essentially remains there forever.) Suppose you are using your ATARI Computer as a word processor to write a paper or report. As you type in new material it appears on the screen. It is also stored in RAM memory. As you edit the document the material in RAM changes to reflect your modifications. Suppose now that it is late at night and you decide to stop, get some sleep, and finish it in the morning. You could leave the computer on all night, but if the power went off even for a second everything in RAM would be lost. All you need to do to avoid that very unpleasant possibility, is to tell the computer to *save* your work on a diskette. You might use an instruction like this: SAVE:"D1: Chapter 1" which means "save the material I have typed on the diskette in drive 1 under the name 'Chapter 1'." Now with a copy of the material on the diskette you can switch the computer off and sleep peacefully. The next morning it is only necessary to insert the correct diskette into the disk drive and tell the computer to load the material named "Chapter 1" back into RAM.

The ATARI 400 Home Computer comes with 16K of RAM installed inside the computer. Although some accessory manufacturers market boards that will increase the amount of RAM in the ATARI 400 Computer to 32K, the computer was designed to remain permanently a computer with 16K RAM. The ATARI 800 computer, on the other hand, has several expansion slots where extra memory cartridges can be placed. The computer comes with 16K of RAM. RAM can be increased to 48K simply by plugging in extra RAM modules. One company that makes accessories for ATARI Computers is even advertising an attachment that permits you to use over 200K of RAM! That much RAM, however, must be housed in a box that is connected to the computer by cable.

I/O Ports

A *port* is a sort of gate or entryway into the computer. Data flows into and out of the computer through a variety of I/O or input/output ports. These ports generally consist of some electronic circuits and a plug or connection that mates the computer with another device such as a printer or a television screen.

Video display ports. It requires quite a lot of hardware and software to display the data stored in a computer's memory in orderly rows on a video screen. Most computers will display at least 24 lines of 40 characters or 16 lines of 62 characters on a television screen or video monitor. Most computers also permit you to display a variety of graphic figures and symbols. Graphic figures can be combined to create pictures, charts, and illustrations. Some computers have special circuits that give them very sophisticated graphics features. The ATARI Computers achieve superior color graphics by using special circuits, like those in the ATARI arcade games, to put brilliant color displays on your color television screen.

Cassette I/O. The least expensive method of storing computer data is a good tape recorder. All the major small computers currently available have built-in cassette I/O features. The cassette system converts all the little ASCII bits and bytes into tones which are stored on tape. To put this taped data back into the computer's memory you reverse the process. The tones on the tape are converted back into 1s and 0s, collected into bytes, and stored in RAM.

Disk I/O. This is really a special version of a serial I/O but it is important enough to be treated separately. Like many small computers, the ATARI 800 Computer has provisions for storing programs and data on cassette and on *floppy diskettes.* A user can store over 80,000 bytes of information on each 5¼-inch floppy disk using the ATARI 810 Disk Drive. A floppy diskette looks a lot like a thin 45 RPM record enclosed in a protective envelope. The *platter* inside the envelope is covered with a magnetic coating that can be magnetized by a recording head inside the disk drive. As the drive spins the floppy diskette, the head presses against the platter and reads the information stored on it or writes new information on it. Data can be saved on, and retrieved from, the diskette very quickly. The speed of operation plus its high degree of reliability makes a disk drive essential for many business and professional applications and for home applications that require manipulation of large amounts of financial information. You can connect up to four disk drives to the ATARI 800 Computer. It is possible to connect up to four disk drives to the ATARI 400 Computer as well.

Serial and parallel I/O. There are two types of *general purpose* I/O ports in small computers. These ports are called parallel and serial. A parallel port has a wire or connection for each of the eight bits in a byte of data. If you tell the computer to send a byte out of a parallel port to a printer, the eight bits in a byte are all shipped out to the printer at the same time over eight different lines. Input from the keyboard to the computer also generally takes place through a parallel port. Printers, modems or telephone couplers, music synthe-sizers, and many other devices can be attached to either a serial or a parallel port.

Serial I/O ports work a bit differently from parallel ports. When eight bits of data arrive at a serial port, they don't all leave at the same time. Instead, the first bit in a byte is sent out on one line, then the next bit goes out on the same line, and so on. All the bits in each byte march out of the computer (or into the computer) over the same line. Any work that in-volves transmitting data over telephone lines will use a serial port.

The term *baud rate* is often used in relation to serial ports. Telephone couplers (modems) generally work at a speed of *300 baud.* Simply defined, a baud rate of 300 is equivalent to a speed of 300 bits per second (around 350 words per minute). Last year we bought a small printer that could be connected to a serial I/O port. Since our computers all had serial I/O ports we assumed it would plug right in. Unfortunately, the fine print in the printer manual told us it accepted data only at a speed of 600 baud while several of our computers trans-mitted at 300 or 1200, but not 600. Like the man said, let the buyer beware.

The ATARI Computers have a simple serial I/O port built in. It can be used to connect either of the ATARI 40 character printers to the computer. (A 40 character printer is one that will print up to 40 characters on each line.) The more sophis-ticated ATARI 825 80-Column Printer cannot be connected to a serial port; it requires a parallel port. The optional ATARI 850 Interface Module can be used with both the ATARI 400 and ATARI 800 Computers. It has a standard parallel port for a printer. It also has four sophisticated serial I/O ports that can be used to connect modems and/or serial printers to the computer. The serial I/O ports on the Interface Module meet the RS-232C standards, which means you can probably con-nect printers made by many different manufacturers to your ATARI Computer if they also have a serial I/O port that meets the widely accepted RS-232C standard.

Game paddle and joystick I/O ports. These are all spe-cial versions of a parallel I/O port designed specifically for a particular device. Computers that have such ports are more versatile. The ATARI Computer has provisions for connecting up to four different controller devices. Joystick controllers and game paddles are both available as options.

CPU

The CPU, or central processing unit, is the heart of a computer system. Although most CPU chips are smaller than an Oreo cookie, the electronic components they contain would have filled a room a few decades ago. Using advanced micro-electronic techniques, manufacturers can cram thousands of circuits into tiny silicon chips that work dependably and use less power than an electric razor. There are several manufacturers of CPU chips. Intel makes the 8080, the 8085, and several others. Zilog makes the Z80 and the Z-8000; Motorola makes the 6800; and MOS Technology makes the 6502 used in the ATARI Computers. While there are real differences among the CPU chips mentioned above, the differences are mainly of interest to computer designers and experienced programmers. You can work with your computer a long time without even knowing which chip it uses. (Do you know what type of engine you have in your car?) You don't need to know anything about the internal workings of your computer either.

Regardless of the chip, the CPU does all the actual processing inside the computer. It also sends signals to the other parts of the computer which synchronize the operation of each component. This synchronization permits the system to perform thousands of operations a second. These operations are fairly simple (e.g. adding two numbers together) but the speed at which they are done allows the computer to do some very complex things by breaking down complicated jobs into hundreds of simple steps.

Again, if this brief introduction to computer hardware has caught your interest, there are several very good books in the dilithium Press catalog which provide more information.

Chapter 13

The Current Crop

We subscribe to over 50 computer periodicals and attend our share of conventions, conferences, and trade shows. A rough guess would be that through these various outlets computer manufacturers announce two or three new systems a month. The companies that offer these new machines to the public range in size from billion dollar conglomerates to one-person operations occupying half of a two-car garage. The products offered enter a marketplace where there is already a large assortment of equipment. The abundance makes choosing a computer difficult, but it also means you are more likely to find a system that fits your needs.

During 1979-81 there were, to be sure, some failures in the small computer marketplace. Names like MITS, Digital Group, Sphere, and Processor Technology are gone now. But for every computer manufacturer that disappeared, at least four or five new players tossed their chips into the pot. Names like Atari, Sinclair, Sylvania, Mattell, Quasar, Sharp, MicroExpander, Matsushita, and Texas Instruments are heard more and more often these days.

With all the models available today we would need a whole book just to describe each model. In this chapter we have, of necessity, focused our attention on the small computers you are most likely to see in retail outlets near you.

The charts* which follow this introduction allow you to comparatively evaluate the popular models on many different variables – from size of display to types of accessories available. Before presenting the chart, however, some explanation is required. The chart is divided into eight major areas of interest: Video Display, Sound, Keyboard, Technical Specifications, Accessories, User Friendliness, Service, and After Sale Support. Each major area is broken down into more specific categories. There are a lot of items that you will need to consider. We have tried to include most of them. To make the charts readable we have abbreviated wherever possible. Here is a brief explanation of what each category means.

VIDEO DISPLAY

TV – Can the computer use a standard television as a video display? If the answer is *YES*, you can take your computer out of the box and hook it up to your TV. If the answer is *PM*, you will have to buy a special RF modulator before you can use the computer with a standard television. If the answer is *NO*, either the computer or the television will require modification.

Monitor – Can the computer use a monitor as a video display? If the answer is *YES*, the computer will hook to a monitor with no special modification. However, you may have to buy a special cable. If the answer is *BI*, the monitor is built into the computer console.

Maximum Character Display – How many lines of how many characters can be displayed at once? For instance, 24×40 means that the computer will display 24 lines of 40 characters or 960 characters.

Screen Editing Capability – Some computers do not permit you to correct errors once you type something and it appears on the screen. The only alternative is to type the entire line over again. Other computers have special keys and special commands that permit you to correct, modify, and *edit* material after it has been typed into the computer. There are several codes in this column. *ID* means that you can insert or

---

*The information contained in this chapter is based on facts contained in operation manuals, catalog advertisements and product sheets which are reasonably believed to be accurate as of the date of printing of this book.

delete material in a line. Does the computer tell you when you've made a programming mistake or do you have to run the program first? An *SE* indicates that the computer provides an immediate error message when you make the error. *FC* means that the computer has full cursor control. This means that you can move the cursor around the screen using only the control key and the arrow keys. *PC* is partial cursor control. This means that the cursor can be moved but it requires a group of keys rather than just the control key and an arrow key. *OW* is overwrite. This is the ability to write over material on the screen. *LB* is a line buffer. A line buffer lets you store a line while you are working on it. For instance, assume you want to have two lines that say almost the same thing. You can write the first one and then make only those changes you want for the second line. The computer will save both lines. Suppose you have this line

100 IF R = 100 THEN GOTO 200

If you also want a line that says:

110 IF R = 200 THEN GOTO 300

all you have to do is change the numbers. A line buffer is an absolute must for most business applications.

Color

Number of Colors – Some computers only display black and white, some display a few colors, and some can put a rainbow to shame.

Background Change – Can the computer change the background color without disturbing the color of any text or graphics being displayed?

Change Text Color – Can the color of the material being displayed be changed without changing the background color?

Graphics

Text Modes – Many computers can display only one size of character on the screen. Others offer two or more sizes. *NT* is normal type. *LT* is large type and *ET* is extra large type.

Total Number of Graphics Modes – Computers with the ability to create graphics as well as text displays vary in the

ATARI 400 Home Computer

ATARI 830 Acoustic Modem

*ATARI 850
Interface Module*

ATARI 800 Computer

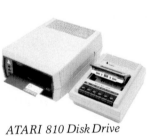

*ATARI 810 Disk Drive
ATARI 410 Program Recorder*

*ATARI 825
80-Column Printer*

ATARI 820 40-Column Printer

ATARI 822 Thermal Printer

number of graphics modes available. A computer with one graphics *mode* can display only one type and size of graphics. Usually one mode systems have relatively coarse graphics that do not permit you to create very fine grained graphics displays. A circle, for example, may be somewhat sawtoothed in appearance rather than smooth. A few computers have several graphics modes. They are usually capable of displaying a variety of graphics styles which range from simple and coarse to complex and precise or *fine grained.*

Highest Resolution Possible – Graphics involves the ability to independently manipulate different sections of the video display. A computer that lets you divide the screen into 600 little squares, and control each one without affecting another one, can create a higher quality of graphics than a computer that divides the same screen area into only 300 squares. *Resolution* thus refers to the quality of the display. The larger the number of independently controlled spots on the screen (and thus the smaller each one of them is) the higher the resolution.

Additional Graphics Capabilities – Some computers have special features that make it possible to create very sophisticated graphics. The key answers here are PM, PD and RV. *PM* means that the computer has player missile graphics. This feature allows you to do animation. *PD,* or programmable display list, lets you use more than one graphics mode at a time. Reverse video, or *RV,* is the ability of the computer to display dark characters on a light background.

SOUND CAPABILITIES

Cassette Recorder to TV Sound – Can the computer take an audio signal from a track on its tape recorder and play it through the television speaker?

Automatic Volume Control – Does the tape system used have a built-in volume control rather than a user adjusted volume control? An automatic control helps insure that programs and data you store on a cassette will be recorded properly.

Small Speaker in Computer – Does the computer incorporate a speaker that can be used to generate sound? This is a very important *user friendliness* feature. Can the computer warn you orally if you make a mistake?

Volume Levels – How many volume levels are under computer control?

Number of Voices – Can the computer divide sound into chords? If so, how many chords or *voices* are available?

Number of Different Musical Notes – This indicates how much variability is possible.

Number of Tonal Qualities – Pure notes are one thing. In reality, many sounds owe their appeal to distortions or variations from the *pear-shaped* sound of a pure note. Some computers can vary tonal qualities as well as the musical note itself.

KEYBOARD

Letter Case – Does the computer display just upper case, *U*; or, does it display both upper and lower case, *B.*

Number of Special Function Keys – On some keyboards there are special keys which can be used to issue common commands (e.g. System Reset, Insert). Computers without special function keys may require you to push two or even three keys simultaneously or in sequence to issue a command.

Number of Special Graphics Characters – In addition to letters, numbers, and punctuation marks, some computers assign special graphics characters to some keys. These symbols may include anything from Greek letters to clubs, spades, hearts, and diamonds. Graphics characters are very handy.

Total Number of Keys – Can the computer do a variety of things with a key or does every function require a special key? Fifty to sixty keys is a good number here.

Full-Size Typewriter-Style Keyboard – Does the computer have a standard keyboard similar to those on an office typewriter?

Pressure-Sensitive (Membrane) Keyboard – Does the computer have a sealed, pressure-sensitive keyboard?

TECHNICAL SPECIFICATIONS

Main Processor Chip – Which chip (e.g. 280, 8080, 6502, 6800) does the computer use?

Custom LSI Chips Used – Does the computer use any special LSI (large scale integrated) circuits to enhance the operation of the system? Custom chips can be used to create graphics, show color, etc. A computer without the custom chips may require a lot of sophisticated graphics programming.

RAM (Minimum-Maximum) – How much user programmable memory is available in the basic system? What is the maximum amount of memory available in a fully expanded system?

BASIC Removable – Is BASIC, the most popular computer language, permanently installed in the computer? In some systems as much as 10 to 16K of memory space is permanently occupied by BASIC. That means the space is used by BASIC even when you are not using BASIC. A better approach is to put BASIC in a cartridge which can be removed when BASIC is not needed. That leaves more room for other uses in the memory map.

Expandability

Input/Output Ports – Are ports available for devices such as serial and parallel printers?

Special Interface Cards Required for Adding Accessories – Does the computer require you to add special circuits to the computer before devices such as printers can be used?

ACCESSORIES AVAILABLE

RS232C Port – Can the computer be hooked up to equipment manufactured by other companies? If it has an RS232 port, it probably can.

Are these accessories available from the manufacturer: Monitor, Cassette Recorder, Disk Drive, Printer and Modem? The answer will be either *NO* or a number. The number indicates how many different items are available. For example, a 3 in the printer column indicates that the company manufactures three different printers.

Input Accessories Available – Can Joystick Controllers (JC), Paddle Controllers (PC), and Keyboard controllers (KC) be used with the computer?

USER FRIENDLINESS

Cartridge Programs Available – The easiest way to change programs in a computer is via cartridge. To change programs just pull out one cartridge and insert another. Programs come packaged on tape, disk, or in cartridges. Both tapes and disk are harder to use than cartridges.

Protected Doomsday Keys – Are keys that could wipe out your program isolated or protected so that it is difficult to inadvertently press them?

Safety Features

Built-In TV Protection – Does the computer provide a means of protecting the television screen from being *burned* permanently if a static display is left on the screen for a long period of time?

Protected Circuit Boards – It should not be easy for prying fingers to get into the computer and investigate circuit boards. Board should be protected by enclosures and/or covers that require tools to remove.

Accessories Added Without Exposing Delicate Computer Parts – Can you plug in a disk drive or a printer without going inside the computer?

Memory Added Without Exposing Delicate Computer Parts – Can you add memory to the computer without going inside the computer?

Accessories Added With Easily Identified Cables – It should be easy to determine which cable goes with which accessory.

SERVICE

Manufacturer Service Centers – Does the manufacturer have support centers which provide repair services for the computer?

Servicing Dealer Network – Are dealers able to provide on-site repair service for the computer?

AFTER SALE SUPPORT

Magazine for Owners – Does the manufacturer publish a magazine for owners? Q is quarterly, S is semi-annually and V is infrequently.

User Group Support Program – Does the manufacturer provide support for user groups?

Toll Free Customer Support Number – Does the manufacturer provide a toll free number owners can call for information and assistance?

	ATARI® 400™ COMPUTER	ATARI® 800™ COMPUTER	TEXAS INSTRUMENTS 99/4A
COMPUTER VIDEO DISPLAY			
TV	Yes	Yes	PM
Monitor	No	Yes	Yes
Maximum character display	24 × 40	24 × 40	24 × 32
Screen editing capability	LB, FC, ID, OW, SE	LB, ID, OW, FC, SE	O
Color			
Number of colors	128	128	16
Background change	Yes	Yes	Yes
Change text color	Yes	Yes	Yes
Graphics			
Text modes	NT, LT, ET	NT, LT, ET	1
Total number of graphics modes	11	11	2
Highest resolution possible	320 × 192	320 × 192	192 × 256
Additional graphics capabilities	PM, PD, RV	PM, PD, RV	PM
SOUND CAPABILITIES			
Cassette recorder to TV sound	Yes	Yes	No
Automatic volume control	Yes	Yes	No
Small speaker within computer	Yes	Yes	No
Volume levels	16	16	30
Number of voices	4	4	3*
Number of different musical notes	256	256	5
Number of different tonal qualities (distortion)	8	8	2
KEYBOARD			
Letter case	B	B	B
Number special function keys	4	4	0
Number of special graphics characters	29	29	0
Total number of keys	61	61	48
Full-size typewriter-style keyboard	No	Yes	No
Pressure-sensitive (membrane)	Yes	No	No

*Plus separate tone generator

TRS-80 COLOR COMPUTER	TRS-80 MODEL III	COMMODORE PET 4000	COMMODORE VIC 20	APPLE II PLUS
Yes	No	No	PM	PM
No	BI	BI	Yes	Yes
16 × 32	16 × 64	40 × 25	22 × 23	24 × 40
FC	PC, LB, ID, OW	ID, FC, OW	FC, ID, OW SE	PC, SE
8	0	0	16	16
Yes	No	No	Yes	No
No	No	No	Yes	No
1	2	1	1	1
6	1	1	3	3
192 × 256	128 × 48	80 × 50	176 × 176	280 × 192
RV	No	No	RV	RV
No	No	No	No	No
No	No	No	Yes	No
No	No	Yes	No	Yes
0	No	No	0	1
1	0	0	4	1
255	0	0	21	32
0	0	0	1	16
U	B	B	B	B
0	0	7	4	0
0	64	4	62	0
53	65	74	66	51
Yes	Yes	Yes	Yes	Yes
No	No	No	No	No

	ATARI® 400™ COMPUTER	ATARI® 800™ COMPUTER	TEXAS INSTRUMENTS 99/4A
TECHNICAL SPECIFICATIONS			
Main microprocessor chip (eg. 6502)	6502B	6502B	9900
Custom LSI chips used	Yes	Yes	Yes
RAM (minimum-maximum)	16K-16K	16K-48K	16K-48K[1]
BASIC removable	Yes	Yes	No
Expandability			
Input/Output ports	5	5	3
Special interface cards required for adding accessories	No	No	No
ACCESSORIES AVAILABLE			
RS232C Port	Yes	Yes	Yes
Monitor	No	Yes	Yes[2]
Cassette recorder	Yes	Yes	Yes
Disk Drive	Yes	Yes	Yes
Printer	3	3	Yes
Modem	Yes	Yes	Yes
Input accessories available	JC, PC, KC	JC, PC, KC	JC, PC
USER FRIENDLINESS			
Cartridge programs available	Yes	Yes	Yes
Protected **doomsday keys**	Yes	Yes	Yes
Safety Features			
Built-in television protection	Yes	Yes	No
Protected circuit board	Yes	Yes	Yes
Accessories added without exposing delicate computer parts	Yes	Yes	Yes
Memory added without exposing delicate computer parts	Yes	Yes	Yes
Accessories added with easily identified cables	Yes	Yes	Yes

[1] Standard BASIC will not access all 48K of memory.
[2] 10″ color monitor.

TRS-80 COLOR COMPUTER	TRS-80 MODEL III	COMMODORE PET 4000	COMMODORE VIC 20	APPLE II PLUS
6809	Z80	6502	6502	6502
No	0	0	Yes	0
4K-32K	4K-48K	16K-32K	5K-32K	16K-48K
No	No	No	Yes	No
1	3	5	3	0
Yes	Yes	No	No	Yes
Yes	Yes	Yes	Yes	Yes
No	Yes	B1	Yes	Yes[3]
Yes	Yes	Yes	Yes	Yes
Yes	Yes	Yes	Yes	Yes
2	3	Yes	Yes	3
Yes	Yes	Yes	Yes	Yes
JC	No	0	0	PC, JC[4]
Yes	No	No	Yes	No
Yes	No	No	No	No
No	No	No	No	No
Yes	Yes	Yes	Yes	No
No	Yes	Yes	No	No
No	No	No	No	No
No	Yes	No	Yes	Yes

[3] Black and white only; color is available from another source.
[4] A graphics tablet is also available.

	ATARI® 400™ COMPUTER	ATARI® 800™ COMPUTER	TEXAS INSTRUMENTS 99/4A
SERVICE			
Manufacturer service centers	Yes	Yes	Yes
Servicing dealer network	Yes	Yes	No
AFTER-SALE SUPPORT			
Magazine for owners	Q	Q	No
Users group support program	Yes	Yes	No
Toll-free customer support number	Yes	Yes	Yes

TRS-80 COLOR COMPUTER	TRS-80 MODEL III	COMMODORE PET 4000	COMMODORE VIC 20	APPLE II PLUS
Yes	Yes	Yes	Yes	Yes
Yes	Yes	No	Yes	Yes
Q	Q	No	Yes	V
Yes	No	No	Yes	Yes
Yes	Yes	Yes	Yes	Yes

At the end of the book, we have included a group of cards that will help you decide which computer is best for you. There is a card for each major area of interest: home use, business applications, education and communications.

Chapter 14

Where To Find Everything
We Didn't Tell You

It is said that an army travels on its stomach. The analogy for computer users might be that their progress is determined by their sources of information. You, of course, are ahead of the game since you had the good taste to read this book. It has provided you with a solid foundation of essential information.

This book, however, is just a beginning. Learning more about computers is a difficult process for two main reasons. First, the field is changing rapidly. In all likelihood some of the things in this book will have changed by the time you read it. Many changes will have occurred since we began writing. For example, the technology of data storage has advanced so quickly that many books written just a year or two ago do not deal with important topics such as hard disk systems, backup storage options, and quad-density or double-sided disk drives.

A second problem that plagues us in this field is the technical nature of the wide range of information available. You cannot become an expert in every area of knowledge about small computers. It is just not possible. There is too much to know, it changes too quickly, and it is not possible to keep all the knowledge fresh by using it every day. The day of the all-around computer user who could write programs, build and repair equipment, and use the computer to do a job is just about over. Most users want to treat their computers just like they do a typewriter or any other office machine. They learn to operate it and leave the repair, maintenance, and improvements to someone else.

Since a computer can be programmed to do many different jobs it will be profitable to learn something about computer languages, different programs that can be bought and used on your computer, and different types of accessories that are available. It will pay, though, to spend some time thinking through just what you want to learn. Is hardware and equipment your bag? Is learning to write your own software an interest? Do you want to concentrate on one particular computer and learn everything you can about it? Is there one special area such as word processing, accounting, statistics, or computer-assisted instruction that interests you? The answers to questions such as these will help determine the next step in your learning program. This chapter will also help by describing some of the typical sources of information on small computers.

BIBLIOGRAPHIES AND DIRECTORIES

Without reservation we would recommend that you buy the *Periodical Guide for Computerists.* It is a yearly guide published by E. Berg Publications, P.O. Box 1151, Bothell, WA 98011. The price is very reasonable, and you get a bibliographic guide to all the material that appeared in the major computer magazines and journals during the year. If, for example, you're considering buying a particular computer system, the *Guide* will tell you where to find reviews of the equipment. Looking for a program to do a particular job? The *Guide* can help you by providing information on programs published in magazines and tell you where to find reviews of commercial software, too.

There are also several directories of computer programs for particular computers. The magazine *Micro* publishes a list of software for computers using the 6502 microprocessor chip (e.g. ATARI Computers). The 6502 software list is a continuing feature of the magazine, which means you'll have to buy the magazine, including back issues, to get an up-to-date list. For some, the list will be worth the price of the magazine (available from Micro INK Inc., Chelmsford, MA 01824).

BOOK PUBLISHERS

It is true that some of the big name or general purpose publishing houses are involved in producing books for small-computer users. Prentice Hall, for example, has a number of books about microcomputers, but most of them are written for professionals with degrees in electrical engineering or computer science. John Wiley & Sons has a series of paperbacks that are specifically directed to the beginner, with many of them written by well-known authors in the small-computer field.

For most of the big general purpose publishers, however, books about small computers are a sideline. Their main interest is somewhere else. There are six book publishers, though, who have committed a large amount of their corporate energy to publishing material for small-computer users. Our publisher, dilithium Press, (P.O. Box 606, Beaverton, OR 97075) has a list of over 80 books, all of them on some aspect of small computing. We may be a little prejudiced, but we believe dilithium has the best line of small-computer books on the market. The difficulty level of dilithium's books ranges from introductory to advanced, with an emphasis on the beginning and intermediate levels. The dilithium catalog, *Brain Food,* is a free publication you will find very useful. Write and ask to be put on the mailing list. dilithium also publishes computer programs for several popular computers; they're listed in the catalog, too.

Another important publisher is Hayden Book Company (50 Essex Street, Rochelle Park, NJ 07662). Hayden publishes a variety of books in the electronics field and is an active distributor of computer programs. You will see racks of Hayden software in many computer stores. A similar company familiar to ham radio operators and television repairmen is Howard W. Sams Publishers (4300 W. 62nd Street, Indianapolis, IN 46206). While there are some introductory books in the Sams catalog, many are written for the professional or serious hobbyist who has considerable interest and background in electronics. The Sams books also tend to emphasize circuit design and construction rather than general computer use or software. If you're interested in building your own computer or in designing or building equipment that can be used with your computer then the Sams catalog should be of great interest.

There are three other publishers, Osborne, Sybex, and Scelbi, which should also be mentioned. Adam Osborne is a well-known writer and consultant who started his own publishing house several years ago. Recently, the company became part of the McGraw-Hill empire and is now Osborne/McGraw-Hill (630 Bancroft Wa, Berkeley, CA 94710). The original line of Osborne books were heavy tomes that took great patience and effort (a Ph.D. didn't hurt either) to get through. They were read mainly by a sophisticated audience of engineers and experienced design specialists who were interested in using the new technology in equipment they designed or built. More recently, Osborne has begun to publish some introductory books that may be of interest to the novice. In addition, the company has published several books which consist of listings of programs you can type into your computer and run. Two other publishers, Sybex, Inc., 2344 Sixth Street, Berkeley, CA 94710 and Scelbi Publishers, 20 Hurlbut Street, Elmwood, CT 06110 have a line of books similar to those of Osborne.

Several of the magazines that will be mentioned in later sections also publish books, particularly *Byte* and *Creative Computing*. The management of *Kilobaud* also runs Instant Software, a publishing house with a very nice catalog of computer programs.

Before moving on to other sources of information we should note that most of the major computer magazines carry reviews of books. A thorough review can sometimes be invaluable in helping decide whether a book is worth its price to you. However, be sure that the magazine reflects your technical level. A very sophisticated technical journal such as *Byte* may give an introductory book a poor review ("it's too simple") while a consumer oriented magazine such as *Personal Computing* may think it is just what you need. What the reader of a technical journal thinks is simple and what you think is simple might be two entirely different things.

MAGAZINES

We have divided the magazines into three categories according to the specificity of their coverage. Every computer user will probably find it profitable to subscribe to at least one or two, and many will subscribe to several. Magazines are excellent sources of current, up-to-date information.

General Electronics Magazines

Magazines in this category are not devoted totally to computers, but they have enough articles on computers to make them worthwhile.

Radio-Electronics – This magazine tries to cover many aspects of the electronics field with frequent articles on audio equipment, radio, television (including satellite reception), and video recorders. Most issues include a few *build this* articles. In recent years *Radio-Electronics* has published many good articles on computers. Several of the articles are introductory in nature and up-to-date while a few have described ways of building small computers or computer accessories. Since this magazine is on most newsstands, we suggest you browse through each issue and decide whether it has enough relevant computer information to warrant buying it.

Popular Electronics – Like *Radio-Electronics,* this one also tries to cover the waterfront. The mix of articles in the two magazines is similar. It would be difficult to choose between them since both often have useful information. One thing that might tilt things in favor of *Popular Electronics,* if you're considering subscribing to one or the other, is the fact that two of the regular columns in it are about computers. "Computer Sources" by Leslie Solomon presents a brief description of new computer equipment and software. "Computer Bits" by Carl Warren generally consists of a page or two of commentary about some aspect of small computer use. Warren may also discuss new equipment or software and may even include a program or two for one of the more popular machines. The construction projects described in each issue of *Popular Electronics* are often computer-related as well. Like *Radio-Electronics, Popular Electronics* is available at most newsstands.

Major Computer Magazines.

The periodicals covered in this section are all aimed at the small-computer market. They may vary somewhat in their emphasis, but they all try to cover general developments in the field. A well-stocked computer store will generally carry most current issues of many of these magazines.

Byte – One of the first, *Byte* has become a sophisticated small-computer magazine with articles primarily of interest to the initiated. There are articles on programming languages, many articles that tell you how to build computer equipment, and several regular columns on a variety of topics from education to computer languages. Most beginners will find *Byte* tough sledding. New computer users who already have a strong electronics background, however, may find the construction articles both understandable and interesting. In fact, many consider the series of construction articles written by Steve Ciarcia to be one of *Byte's* greatest contributions to the literature.

Almost 70% of *Byte's* readers are engineers, scientists, or computer programmers and 68% of the readership has at least a bachelor's degree. *Byte* is now a McGraw-Hill magazine that is slick, well edited, and aimed at intermediate and advanced small-computer users.

Microcomputing – Compared to *Byte, Microcomputing* is less cerebral. There are fewer conceptual articles and more *here's how-to-do-it* articles. A recent issue, for example, told you how to turn the Exidy Sorcerer computer into a *dumb terminal* for a time-sharing system, how to build several pieces of computer test equipment, and how to add inexpensive extra memory to the Cosmac Elf computer. The same issue carried general articles on computers in the office, reviews of several new computers, reviews of commercial software packages, and several more construction articles. Since *Microcomputing* always has articles about specific computers, there may be many articles in each issue that do not interest you. The ones on the particular computer you own, however, may be worth far more than the cost of the magazine. The articles in *Microcomputing* range from introductory to very advanced, and the topics vary considerably. There are product reviews, how-to-build-it pieces, articles on different types of computer languages, and actual programs you can type into your computer and run. Few people will be intensely interested in every article, but there are likely to be at least ten or so in each issue of *Microcomputing* that make the issue worth its price. That's especially true if you have interests in both software and hardware.

Interface Age – The cover of this magazine says "computing for the home and business." That is, indeed, where *Interface Age* seems to concentrate. Unlike *Microcomputing*, it rarely publishes an article on how to build something. Instead it concentrates on articles of interest to the person who wants to use a computer to do a job. Like *Byte, Interface Age* publishes concept or idea articles as well as several important columns on computers in education, legal issues, and mathematics and computers.

Interface Age is probably the magazine most suitable for the small-business person and the home computer owner with interests in applications. By this we mean the person interested in programming the computer but not in building equipment or repairing sick systems. *Interface Age* has articles on programming, it regularly publishes programs readers can use in their own computers, and it has some of the best reviews published. *Interface Age* publishes reviews on computers, computer systems, accessory boards, and software packages. *IA* also has a large "New Products Directory" section that includes both hardware and software for small computers. It has to be considered one of the better magazines for its target audience.

Popular Computing – The editors of *Byte* correctly surmised that the level of most articles appearing in *Byte* is well beyond the comprehension of most beginners. Not wanting to ignore the needs of a large segment of the market, they created *Popular Computing*. It is a mixture of tutorial articles, product reviews, and application descriptions that seem particularly suited to the needs and interests of relatively inexperienced computer users. Most *Popular Computing* articles can be understood by readers with little or no background in the area of computers. That one attribute makes *Popular Computing* a logical choice for most people reading this book. That is not to say the articles talk down to the reader; they just don't assume you have a Ph.D. in computer science.

Personal Computing – This magazine covers some of the same territory as *Interface Age*. While the format of *Personal Computing* is a bit less formal or businesslike, it regularly publishes articles of interest to the small-business person. There will probably be more reviews of expensive business computers and software in *Interface Age* and more *fun* programs in *Personal Computing.* A recent issue of *Personal Computing,* for example, included a BASIC program to print price lists for products with a *two-step distribution channel* and another BASIC program that will let you be Alice searching for the Rabbit with the mean Queen and dippy Mad Hatter interfacing with your efforts. *Personal Computing* also publishes many programs for home and school applications (e.g. a grading program for teachers and a program to balance your checkbook). Reviews of new products and listings of programs you can type in and use are *Personal Computing'*s strong points. *Personal Computing* also has regular columns on computer chess, computer bridge, and computer games. It has, in fact, been criticized because it devotes so much space to these topics. Perhaps some issues were heavy on chess, but *Personal Computing* has always published articles of general interest.

Creative Computing – This magazine is a lot like *Personal Computing.* It carries articles that can be understood by the beginner and the intermediate computer user. Most issues are a mixture of product reviews, tutorial articles, and programs. *Creative Computing* has excellent reviews of computers and computer accessories. It does a good job of reviewing software packages as well. Another strong point of *Creative Computing* is the sophisticated software provided. It has published hundreds of computer games, simulations, and applications programs. Some of their programs are just plain fun, but many *Creative Computing* programs are educational (e.g. a program to teach children to solve math word problems) or applications (e.g. a program to help department heads manage their budgets). Whereas *Personal Computing* has special columns on chess and bridge, *Creative Computing* has monthly columns on several small computers, including ATARI Computers. These columns are usually only a page or two, but they are extremely helpful to owners of those systems.

Infoworld – *Infoworld* is different from any of the publications mentioned thus far. To begin with, it is published 52 times a year, and it is in a newspaper format. *Infoworld* concentrates on two types of information – news and product reviews. The news includes anything from a blow-by-blow account of corporate mergers, suits, and countersuits, to in-depth pieces on new areas of application (e.g. computers and satellite communication channels) and descriptions of new products. *Infoworld* is targeted for an audience which no other publication serves. Perhaps it's stretching it a bit to call it the *Wall Street Journal* of small computing, but there are similarities.

If you're not interested in *news*, this publication may still be of interest. It carries some of the most critical reviews in the field. If a new and expensive piece of software is poorly writ-ten, if it doesn't do what it claims to do, the *Infoworld* re-viewers say so. They don't mince words. The letters they published on one manufacturer told such a tale of horror that many potential buyers changed their minds. To be fair, *Info-world* also publishes rebuttal letters from the companies in-volved, but all that butting and rebutting frequently gener-ates quite a bit of heat. If you're likely to be buying a lot of ex-pensive software or if you regularly purchase small-computer equipment for your business, a subscription to *Infoworld* is well worth its price.

Special-Purpose Computer Magazines

All of the magazines described thus far are to a greater or lesser extent *general* interest magazines. As the field has grown, however, many small publications aimed at a particu-lar audience have appeared. Some of these publications con-centrate on a particular area of application such as education or small businesses. Others concentrate on one computer or a particular type of computer. The publications in this category tend to come and go at an alarming rate, so be sure the one you're interested in is still publishing before sending in your subscription check.

Applications Magazines

There are two well-established magazines which deal with a particular application. *Small Business Computers* (33 Wat-chung Plaza, Montclair, NJ 07042) publishes articles of inter-est to the business community. Rather than publishing pro-grams that can be used in business, *Small Business Computers* offers tutorial articles (e.g. a guide to small-business computing), articles on special topics (e.g. disk equipment for business), and guides to equipment and programs used by the business community (e.g. current software for mailing lists and labels).

The other popular special-purpose magazine is *The Computing Teacher* (c/o Computing Center, EOSC, LaGrande, OR 98750) which publishes articles on the use of computers at all educational levels. Some programs, usually written in BASIC, are published, but the emphasis is on articles written by educators to describe the way they use computers or their views on the current educational computing scene.

Product-Oriented Publications

A few of the computer manufacturers publish newsletters or magazines about their product. Atari, Inc., for example, publishes a quarterly magazine, *THE ATARI CONNECTION*. All new owners of ATARI Home Computers who return their warranty cards receive a complimentary copy of *THE ATARI CONNECTION* and an offer to subscribe to it. *THE ATARI CONNECTION* contains articles on interesting applications for ATARI Computers, descriptions of new products for ATARI Computers, listings of programs which can be run on the computer, and other information of interest to ATARI Computer owners, as well as a catalog of gift items, such as T-shirts.

In addition to the in-house publications mentioned above, there are several other magazines that deal with only one type of computer.

Compute! (P.O. Box 5406, Greensboro, NC 27403) bills itself as *The Journal for Progressive Computing* and concentrates on the ATARI Computers and six other computers that use the 6502 microprocessor chip. This magazine is one we recommend strongly for ATARI Computer owners. It is attractively produced and regularly prints reviews of accessories for the ATARI Computers, programs that can be typed into your computer and run, and *tutorial* articles that go into the finer points of using the ATARI Computers. A recent issue contained a program for generating large *banner* messages on the screen with an ATARI Computer, a program that let you use the computer as a terminal, instructions for connecting a printer to the computer, a review of the Music is not the only magazine that concentrates on 6502 computers, however.

Micro– The magazine *Micro* is subtitled *The 6502 Journal,* *Micro* (Chelmsford, MA 01824) contains articles on the computers that use the 6502 microprocessor chip. It publishes a mixture of product reviews, construction articles, and programs written in BASIC and 6502 assembly language. *Micro* has grown from a brief offset newsletter with an amateurish appearance to a slick typeset magazine filled with useful information for owners of 6502 computers. Many of the articles assume the reader is an intermediate or advanced computer user.

If you've arrived at this point by reading all the chapters that preceded it, you're at least a bona fide *beginning computer user.* After another book or two mixed with a few subscriptions to some good magazines, you'll fast become an intermediate computer user. Perhaps in a few years we'll even see articles or a book about computers written by you. On the other hand, maybe we won't. Writing books and articles isn't all that much fun. Using computers for fun, for profit, or for learning is a lot more interesting to most people. We hope you join the millions of people who are becoming informed computer users and that you find computers as enjoyable to work with as we do.

Glossary

The purpose of this short glossary is to familiarize you with some of the more common computer terms. Most of these terms are defined elsewhere in this book. Others, however, are not. We have tried to include most of the terms you are likely to encounter in magazines, advertising literature, other books, etc. Please bear in mind that this is a user's glossary, not a dictionary. Our reason for defining these terms is to help you understand the currently available literature. We have taken quite a bit of liberty with some of the definitions. Our emphasis has been on usability rather than completeness. In addition, we have tried to define things only once. Consequently, if we use an abbreviation, we describe it rather than define it; i.e. CPU refers you to Central Processing Unit. If you come across a term that is not defined here you might want to check *Home Computers: A Beginners Glossary and Guide* by Charles Sippl and Merl Miller.

Access time: The length of time it takes for information to be written to or read from a diskette.

Accumulator: A holding register in the computer's arithmetic logic unit that holds instructions for I/O operations. It performs arithmetic operations.

adata: ATASCII Data. Any ATASCII data except commas or carriage returns.

Address: A number or name that identifies a particular location in memory, in a register, or other data source or depository.

aexp: Arithmetic expression

ALGOL: ALGOrithmic Language, a high level language for scientific applications.

Alphameric: Alphanumeric

Alphanumeric: Data presented in both alphabetic and numeric form, for instance a mailing list. The numbers 0-9 and the letters A-Z or any combination thereof.

ALU: Arithmetic Logic Unit

aop: Arithmetic operator

Arithmetic expression: An expression consisting only of numbers and operators, for instance $2+3$.

Arithmetic logic unit: The device within the CPU that performs all of the arithmetic operations: i.e., addition, subtraction, multiplication, division.

Arithmetic operator: A symbol that tells the computer to perform an arithmetic operation. The operators are: + addition; − subtraction; *multiplication; /division; and ^exponentiation (raise to a power).

Arithmetic variable: A location where a numeric value is stored.

Array: A one-dimensional set of elements arranged in tabular form.

ASCII: A simple code system that converts symbols and numbers into numeric values the computer can understand. For instance, when you type *a* on the keyboard of your computer, the number 00100001 is sent to the CPU. (The binary number 01100001 is the decimal number 97.)

Assembler: A program that translates higher-level language code into machine language.

Assembly language: A programming language that uses mnemonic symbols. An assembler converts the mnemonics into machine language.

ATASCII: Atari Inc. version of standard ASCII code. Atari needs an enhanced version due to the greater graphics capability.

Audio track of cassette: A separate track of the cassette that allows the computer to play music, voices, etc.

avar: Arithmetic variable.

BASIC: Beginner's All-purpose Symbolic Instruction Code, a high level computer language designed for beginners. The most common microcomputer language.

Baud: A unit of information transfer. In microcomputers, the baud is defined as bits per second.

Baud rate: The rate at which information is transferred. For instance, a 300 baud rate is 300 bits per second.

Binary number: A number system that uses only two digits, 0 and 1, to express all numeric values. See digital computer.

Bit: The basic unit of computer memory. It is short for binary digit and can have a value of either 1 or 0.

Boot: This is the initialization program that sets up the computer when it is turned on.

Branch: A program segment that tells the computer to skip certain line numbers and return to them later.

Break: To interrupt execution of a program. The computer has a control key labelled BREAK.

Buffer: A temporary storage register used to hold data for further processing.

Bug: A problem that causes a program or computer to perform incorrectly or not at all.

Byte: A group of eight bits (or a memory cell that can store eight bits) usually treated as a unit. It takes one byte to store each unit of information. For instance, the word *love* requires four bytes.

CAI: Computer Aided Instruction.

Cartridge: A $2 \times 3 \times \frac{1}{4}$-inch plastic box that contains ROM software for either BASIC or a program such as STAR RAIDERS™.

Cassette drive: A tape cassette machine designed for use with a computer. Cassettes are usually modified audio cassette tape recorders.

Cathode Ray Tube (CRT): The picture tube of a television set. This is the television receiver or monitor that is used to display computer output.

Central Processing Unit (CPU): This is the heart of the computer. It contains the circuits that control the interpretation and execution of instructions.

Chip: A formed piece of silicon or other semiconductor material; an integrated circuit.

Clock: An electronic circuit in a computer that is a source of timing and synchronizing signals.

COBOL: COmmon Business Oriented Language, a high level language generally used with medium-sized or large computers.

Code: A system of symbols and rules for representing, transmitting, and storing information.

Coding: The design of a computer program.

COLOR: This is a BASIC command unique to computers that have color graphics capability. This command tells the computer what color to use.

Color Register: The specific location in the computer's memory that stores a color you want for your program.

Command: An instruction that tells the computer to perform an operation immediately.

Compiler: A computer program that translates high-level language statements into machine language.

Computer: An electronic device that can receive and follow instructions and then use these instructions to perform calculations or compile, select or correlate data. The primary differences between a computer and a calculator is that a computer can manipulate text, display graphics and make decisions.

Computer aided instruction: The process of teaching by computer. This is a system of individualized instruction that uses a computer program as the teaching medium.

Concatenation: The process of joining two or more strings together to form one new longer string.

Console: The keyboard and other devices that make up the control unit of a computer.

CONTROL: A special key unique to computers whose function is similar to a shift key. Pushing the computer's control key in conjunction with another key causes the computer to perform special functions. For instance pushing the control key in conjunction with the up arrow key causes the cursor to move up.

Control character: A special character that is produced when the computer's control key is pressed in conjunction with another key.

Controller: A device that can be attached directly to the computer or to an external mechanical device so that objects on the screen can be moved around. Joysticks and game paddles are both controllers.

CPU: Central Processing Unit

CRT: Cathode Ray Tube

Cursor: The little flashing square on the CRT that indicates where the next character will be displayed.

Daisy wheel printer: A printing machine whose moving head has a number (usually 96) of radial arms or petals with a type character at the end of each.

Data: Any and all items of information—numbers, letters, symbols, facts, statements, etc., which can be processed or generated by a computer.

Data transmission rate: Baud rate.

Debug: To eliminate errors in a computer program or a computer.

Decimal number system: This is the number system you are familiar with, i.e., 0-9.

Delimiter: A character that establishes the beginning or end of a string of data, but is not a part of the data, for instance quotation marks.

Digital: A system that uses the numbers 0 and 1 to represent all the variables involved in calculation. This means that information can be represented by a series of bits.

Digital computer: A computer that uses a series of electronic offs and ons to represent information. These offs and ons are converted to (or from) binary numbers. Microcomputers are digital computers.

Directory: A list of the files on a disk.

Disc: Disk

Disk: A flat, rotating, circular sheet coated with magnetic material that is used to store bits of information.

Disk drive: A magnetic device that reads from or writes to disks. A disk drive has a floating magnetic head that moves across the disk. It also has a motor that rotates the disk.

Diskette: A floppy disk that is 5¼ or 8 inches in diameter (about the size of a 45 rpm record).

Disk file: Organized collections of data stored on disks.

Disk operating system: A program that operates a disk drive.

Documentation: All of the available information about a particular computer, computer program or set of programs. It should include operating instructions, troubleshooting, labeling, etc.

DOS: Disk operating system.

Dot matrix printer: A printer that forms characters as patterns of dots. The dots lie within a grid of definite dimensions, such as 6×9 dots.

Dual density: A technique of writing twice as much information on a diskette.

Edit: To make changes in data or a program.

Electronic mail: Personal or other messages generated on a computer and stored in the memory of another computer at a different location. The computers are connected via phone lines.

Execute: To run a computer program or part of a program.

exp: Any expression, whether sexp or aexp.

Expression: A combination of numbers, variables and operators that can be evaluated to a single number or variable. For instance, $2 + 3$, $A + B$, and $A + 3$ are all expressions.

External memory: Mass storage.

Fetch: The computer process of getting the instruction from memory.

Field: A unit of information that serves as a building block for a record.

File: An organized collection of related records. A payroll file would have a complete payroll record for each employee.

File management subsystem: A program that controls operations performed on a file.

Filespec: File specification

File specification: A string expression that refers to a device such as the keyboard or to a disk file. It contains information on the type of I/O device, etc.

Firmware: A program permanently written to a media. For instance, a ROM cartridge, such as STAR RAIDERS™, is firmware.

Floppy disk: A flexible plastic disk coated with magnetic recording material on which computer data may be stored.

FMS: File management subsystem.

Formatting: The process of organizing a diskette into tracks and sectors so that the computer can write to it.

FORTRAN: FORmula TRANslation. A high-level computer language used for mathematical or engineering applications.

Function key: A keyboard that tells the computer to perform a specific action; i.e., the *esc* key tells the computer to escape the current program and free the computer for other uses.

Graphics: The ability of a computer to show pictures, line drawings, special characters, etc. on the CRT or printer.

Hard copy: A copy of the computer's output printed on paper.

Hard sectored disk: A disk that has the tracks and sectors physically defined. A hard sectored disk has a group of holes that define the sectors.

Hardware: All of the various physical components of a computer system; i.e., the computer itself, the printer, the TV set, etc.

High-level language: A computer language that uses simple English words to represent computer commands. For instance, the command RUN in BASIC tells the computer to run a program.

Home computer: Microcomputer or personal computer.

IC: Integrated Circuit.

Increment: Increase in value by one or more.

Initialize: To set a program element or hardware device to an initial quality (usually zero).

Input: To transfer data from the keyboard, a diskette or a cassette to RAM.

Input device: A device used to enter information into a computer.

Input-output: The process of entering data into or taking it out of a computer.

Input-output device: A device that can either put information into or take information out of a computer.

Instruction: Properly coded information that causes the computer to perform certain operations.

Integrated circuit: A group of components that form a complete miniaturized electronic circuit consisting of a number of transistors plus associated circuits. These components are fabricated together on a single piece of semiconductor material.

Interactive: A computer system that responds immediately to user input.

Interface: A device that allows two other devices to communicate with each other.

Inverse video: A process that allows you to show dark text on a light background on your CRT. Normally light text is shown on a dark background.

I/O: Input-Output

I/O device: Input-output device.

Jack: A plug socket on a computer.

Joystick controller: A box with a movable plastic stick in the top of it. When attached to the computer, the stick makes objects move around on the screen.

K: Kilo

Keyword: A reserved word that has meaning to the computer and therefore cannot be used as a variable name.

Kilo: A prefix meaning 1000. It is abbreviated K. Thus 4K of memory is about 4000 bytes of memory. (It is exactly 4096 bytes, but 4K is a convenient way to keep track of it.)

Language: It means the same thing as human language. The difference is that a computer language allows humans to communicate with a computer.

lexp: Logical expression

Light pen: A hand-held light sensitive device that allows you to write graphic information on the screen. The information is also written into RAM.

lineno: Line number

Line number: A number that defines a line of programming in a high-level language. Each line of the program begins with a line number. The computer executes the program in line number order starting with the lowest number.

Logic: A systemized interconnection of devices in a computer circuit that causes it to perform certain functions.

Logical expression: An expression, such as $A = B$, composed of two arithmetic or string expressions separated by a logical operator. This is very useful in programming when you want the computer to make decisions. For example, assume you want the computer to count to ten and then print hello. You could use the expression IF $A > 9$ THEN PRINT "HELLO".

Logical operator: A symbol that tells the computer to make a comparison. These operators are: $>$ greater than; $<$ less than; and $=$ equals.

LOGO: A high-level language designed at MIT for use in educational settings.

Loop: A series of programming instructions that recycle. The last instruction in the loop tells the computer to return to the first instruction. Intentional loops have some means of escape built into them. Unintentional loops, caused by programmer error, can only be stopped by pressing the break key or turning the computer off.

lop: Logical operator

Machine language: The lowest level language. It is a pattern of binary coding that tells the computer what to do.

Mass storage: The files of computer data that are stored on media other than the computer's main memory (RAM). Examples are: diskettes and cassettes.

Matrix: A set of numbers or terms arranged in rows or columns. See subscripted variable for an example.

Matrix printer: Dot matrix printer.

Matrix variable: Subscripted variable.

Memory: The internal hardware in the computer that stores information for further use.

Menu: A display shown on the CRT that gives you a list of options. You select an option by typing a letter or number and pressing return.

Microcomputer: A fully operational small computer that uses a microprocessor as its CPU.

Microprocessor: A central processing unit contained on a single chip.

Minifloppy: Diskette

Minidisk: Diskette

Missile: An object (two bits wide) that can be moved around the screen.

Mnemonic: A technique or symbol designed to aid the human memory. Mnemonics and mnemonic code mean essentially the same thing.

Mnemonic code: A system of abbreviations, acronyms and symbols designed to replace obscure, complex terms used in preparing assembly language programs.

Modem: A modulating and demodulating device that enables computers to communicate over telephone lines.

Monitor: A television receiver or CRT device used to display computer output.

mvar: Matrix variable

Null string: A string without any characters in it.

Numeric data: Data consisting entirely of numbers.

Operating system: A collection of programs that help you use the computer.

OS: Operating system.

Output: Information or data transferred from the internal memory of the computer to some external device, such as a CRT, a mass storage device or a printer.

Output device: A device used to take information out of a computer.

Paddle controller: A device used to move objects about on a TV screen.

Parallel: The performance of two or more operations or functions simultaneously. For instance, a parallel port accepts all eight bits of a byte at one time. This is the opposite of a serial port that accepts only one bit at a time.

Pascal: A powerful high-level computer language for business and general use. Named for French mathematician and philosopher Blaise Pascal (1623-1662).

PEEK: A BASIC command that tells the computer to look into a specific location in the computer's memory and see what is stored there.

Peripheral: Any I/O device, a printer for instance.

Personal computer: Microcomputer, home computer.

PILOT: (Programmed Inquiry Learning Or Teaching) This is an easy-to-learn, high-level language designed for use by novice computer users. Primarily intended for educational settings.

Pixel: A picture element that is one point on a screen. The size of the pixel depends on the graphics mode being used and resolution capabilities of the computer.

Player: An object (8 bits wide) which can be moved around the screen.

POKE: A BASIC command that tells the computer to put a new number into a specific location in the computer's memory.

Port: A point of access to a computer.

Power supply: A device, consisting of a transformer and other components, that converts household current (115 or 230 volt) to the DC voltage used by a computer.

PRINT: A command to the computer that tells it to display something on the screen or print it out on a printer.

Printer: A device for producing paper copies (hard copy) of the data output by a computer.

Program: An organized group of instructions that tell the computer what to do. The program must be in a language the computer understands.

Program recorder: Cassette drive.

Prompt: A symbol, usually a question mark, appearing on the screen that asks you to enter information.

RAM: Random access memory

Random access memory: This is the read-write memory available for use in the computer. Through random access the computer can retrieve or deposit information instantly at any memory address.

Random number generator: A program statement or a hardware device that provides a number that cannot be predicted. This is very useful in decision-making programs. For instance, using a random number generator, the computer can simulate dice rolls.

Read: The act of taking data from a storage device, such as a diskette, and putting it in the computer's memory.

Read only memory: A random access memory device that has permanently stored information. The contents of this memory are set during manufacture.

Read write memory: A computer memory that you can put data into or take data out of at any time.

Record: An organized block of data, such as all of the payroll information on one person.

Register: A small temporary storage device in the computer. It holds data that the computer is going to use. For instance, a color register holds an assigned color.

Reserved word: Keyword.

Resolution: The number of points (or pixels) you can put on a television screen (or monitor) both vertically and horizontally.

Reverse video: Inverse video.

ROM: Read Only Memory.

SAVE: A command that tells the computer to store the contents of memory on some other media, such as a diskette or cassette.

Screen: A CRT or television screen.

Sector: The smallest block of data that can be written to or read from a disk file.

Semiconductor: A metal or other material (silicon, for example) with properties between those of conductors and insulators. Its electrical resistance can be changed by electricity, light or heat.

Serial: A group of events that happen one at a time in sequence. For instance, a serial interface reads in a byte one bit at a time. Also, magazines are called serials because they are published one at a time on a regular basis.

SETCOLOR: A BASIC command that tells the computer what hue and luminance will be used with a particular color.

sexp: String expression

Silicon: A nonmetallic chemical element resembling carbon. It is more abundant in nature than any element except oxygen. It is used in the manufacture of transistors, solar cells, etc. It combines with oxygen to form several common minerals such as quartz, sand, etc.

Soft sector: A method of making sectors on a disk using information written on the disk. A soft-sectored disk must be formatted before it can be used.

Software: The programs and data used to control a computer.

Sort program: A program that arranges data in a file in a logical or defined sequence (alphabetically, for instance).

SOUND: A BASIC command that tells the computer to generate musical notes and sounds through the audio system of your television.

Special character: A character displayed by the computer that is not a letter or a number; a heart, for instance.

String: String variable.

String variable: A sequential set of letters, numbers and/or characters. It always ends with a $. For instance, if you wanted the computer to remember your name, you could tell the computer A2$ = "your name".

Subroutine: A part of a program that can be executed by a single statement. This is especially useful when you want one part of a program to do something numerous times.

Subscript: A small letter, number or symbol written below the half line. For instance, the 2 in H_2O. Also, the number in parentheses in a subscripted variable.

Subscripted variable: An element of an array or matrix. For instance, a matrix may have four columns A, B, C, D and four rows 1, 2, 3, 4. If you read left to right across the matrix starting with the 1 under the A, the first element is A(1), which has a value of 1; the next element is B(2), which has a value of 2, etc. Here is the matrix:

```
A B C D
1 2 3 4
2 3 4 1
3 4 1 2
4 1 2 3
```

Superscript: A small letter, number or symbol written above the half line. For instance, the ® in ATARI®.

svar: String variable.

System: All of the various hardware components that make the computer usable; i.e., the computer, the printer, the joystick controller, the disk drive, etc.

Text editor: A computer program that allows you to change or modify the contents of memory. It can modify either data or programs.

var: Variable.

Variable: A quantity that can assume any of a given set of values. For instance, assume A is a variable whose value is 1; if you add 3 to it, its value becomes 4.

Window: A portion of the TV display devoted to a specific purpose.

Word: For our purposes, same as byte.

Word processing: A special feature of a computer that allows you to manipulate text. See also word processor.

Word processor: A very special computer program that helps you manipulate text. You can write a document, insert or change words, paragraphs or pages and then print the document letter perfect.

Write: To store data on external media such as diskette or cassette. The expression *write to diskette* means that the information stored in the computer's memory is sent to the diskette where it is stored.

Write protect: When new material is written to a diskette, any old material there is erased. Write protect is a method of fixing the disk so that it can't be written on.

$: When added to a letter (A$, for instance) it signifies that the letter (A, in this case) is the name of a string variable.

+: It means just what you think, add two numbers (or variables) together.

−: Subtract one number (or variable) from another.

∗: Multiply one number (or variable) by another.

/: Divide one number (or variable) by another.

∧: Exponentiation or raise to a power.

=: Equals is kind of tricky. It doesn't really mean *equal to*. In computer usage it means *assigns a value to*. Therefore, you might see something like B = B + 1.

>: Greater than. For instance, 2 > 1.

<: Less than. For instance, 1 < 2.

Index

APEX, 14
ASAP, 14
ASCII, 138
Accessories, 133, 134, 151, 156
Accountant, 121
Accounting, 119
Accounts payable, 105, 111
Accounts receivable, 105, 111
After Sales Support, 153
Airline schedules, 35
Answer, 68
Answer and Originate, 68
Appliance, 11
Art, 1, 55, 79
Assembly language, 128
Associated Press, 39
ATARI, 5, 14, 62, 78, 89, 127
ATARI Newsletter, 55
ATARI Program Exchange, 14
ATARI Software Acquisition
  Program, 14
Attorney, 109
Audio track, 42, 84, 94
Auto answer, 67

BASIC, 6, 12, 20, 40, 118, 126, 132,
  134, 139, 151
Bar graph, 107
Baud, 66, 69
Baud rate, 142
Bit, 138
Books, 8
Break, 67
Brownout, 134
Budgeting, 105, 106
Buffer, 147

Built-in features, 5
Business, 1, 3, 7, 53, 99, 110, 117
Buying steps, 7, 11
Byte, 138
BYTE, 75

CAI, 12, 39, 78
CMI, 86
CMI, 81
CPU, 143
Calculator, 1
Canned programs, 1, 30, 40, 53, 126
Cartridge, 28, 126, 138, 152
Cash flow, 100, 105
Cassette, 22, 141
Cassette recorder, 23, 42
Cells, 138
Central Processing Unit, 143
Checkbook balancing, 31
Chip, 125
CLASSROOM COMPUTER NEWS,
  77
Color, 15, 19, 41, 63, 81, 147
Color display, 15
Color graphics, 93
Color monitor, 42
Communication, 7, 47, 61
CompuServe, 51, 55, 62
COMPUTE!, 17, 28, 62, 93
Computer, accessories, 17
Computer, electronics, 8
Computer Curriculum Corporation,
  74
Computer assisted instruction, 12,
  39, 78, 81
Computer chess, 28

Computer features, 7
Computer literacy, 8, 41, 75, 78
Computer managed instruction, 81
Computer store, 3, 17, 118
Computing, 52
COMPUTING TEACHER, 75
Conduit, 83
Connect time, 52
Consumer, 49, 50, 53
Convenience, 48
Cost, 23, 43, 74, 110
CREATIVE COMPUTING, 17, 28, 58, 62, 93, 94
Creative writing, 79
Cursor, 147

DBMS, 108
Data, 112
Data base, 54
Data registers, 133
Data track, 94
Database management system, 108
Database manager, 118
Decimal align, 103
Dedicated computer, 36
Demonstrated, 121
Department store, 17
Dependability, 74
Desktop computer, 105
Diagnostic testing, 87
Dialog, 58
Disk, 122, 141
Disk drive, 43, 102, 118
Diskette, 114, 141
Display, 15, 19, 41, 63, 122, 146
Documentation, 121
Doctor, 49
Doomsday, 91, 98, 152
Dow Jones, 58
Download, 52
Drill and practice, 81

Edit, 146
Educated guessing, 107
Education books, 77
Education magazines, 75
Education, 1, 7, 51, 71, 72, 86, 119, 126
EDUCATIONAL COMPUTER MAGAZINE, 77
Educational discount, 95
Electronic bulletin board, 49
Electronic information banks, 49
Electronic mail, 48, 49, 50, 54

Electronic publishing, 49
Electronic worksheet, 107
Electronics, 8
Entertainment, 6, 15, 26, 27
Error, 147
Established dealer, 121
European Countries & Capitals, 82
Expansion, 16

Farms, 47
Features, 7, 122
Filter, 135
Financial, 34
Financial modeling, 118
Floppy disk, 23, 141
Football statistics, 50
Free, 61
Friendliness, 5
Full duplex, 66, 68
Future, 48

Galactic cook, 27
Game programs, 1
Games, 53
Garbage scow captain, 27
Glitch, 135
Graphics, 5, 6, 15, 19, 41, 86, 93, 140, 147, 150

Half duplex, 67, 68
Handshaking, 133
Hands on, 17
Hardware, 118
Health, 6, 37
Hearts, 42
High-level language, 128
Hobby, 35
Home computer, 6, 25, 40, 42
Home control, 6, 26
Home of the future, 37
Host computer, 63

I/O, 66, 140, 141
IC, 125
Independent programmer, 14
INFOWORLD, 17
Information, 47, 55, 114
Information management, 48, 49
Input, 93, 130
Integrated circuit, 125, 133
Interface, 7, 66, 151
INTERFACE AGE, 17
Inventory, 112, 119
Investment, 31
Investment portfolio, 43

Keyboard, 15, 21, 42, 122, 150, 154
Keybounce, 21
Kidproof, 94

Language, 1, 12
Language, assembly, 128
Language, high-level, 128
Language, machine, 126
Learning environment, 74
Learning tool, 28
Line voltage, 135
Local computer networks, 59
Lower case letters, 122

MECC, 79
Machine language, 126
Magazines, 8
Magic, 8
Mailing list, 35
Mainframe, 52
Manager, 8, 99, 105, 117, 121
Marketing, 106
Membrane keyboard, 22, 42, 94
Memory, 104, 115, 118, 122, 123, 137, 138, 152
Memory map, 139
Microcomputing, 17
Minnesota Educational Computing Consortium, 79
Mode, 149
Modem, 52, 68, 142
Modularity, 24
Modulator/demodulator, 68
Monitor, 21, 42, 63, 146
Move, 103
Music, 16, 30, 52, 79, 150
Music synthesizers, 142

Network, 48, 67
New York Times – News Summary, 54

Office expense, 108
ON COMPUTING, 53
Operating system, 123, 138
Options, 42
Order entry, 112
Originate, 68
Output, 93
Overwrite, 147

PCNET, 50
Page layout, 104
Papert, Seymour, 81

Parallel, 8
Parallel I/O, 141
Parallel port, 143
Pascal, 126
Payroll, 108, 111
Personal Computer Network, 50, 52, 78
PERSONAL COMPUTING, 17
Personal development, 6, 28
Personal enrichment, 1
Personal finance, 31
Phone line, 49
Pictures, 26
PILOT, 12, 40, 118, 126, 131, 134, 179
PLATO, 74
POPULAR COMPUTING, 17
Port, 140
Power supply, 22, 134
Prestel, 49
Print, 103, 130
Printer, 63, 102, 122, 123, 142
Profession, 8, 99
Professional, 121
Professor, 49
Programmed instruction, 78
Programming, 6, 30, 118, 133, 134, 147, 178
Programs, 98, 125
Programs, canned, 1, 30, 40

RAM, 8, 133, 138, 151
ROM, 8, 133, 138
RS232C, 142, 151
Random access memory, 139
Read only memory, 138
Real estate, 109, 119
Record keeping, 31
Recreation, 25, 35
Recreational computing, 19
Resolution, 149
Resources, 115
Revolution, 71
Ripple, 135
RUN, 2, 130

SRA, 83
Safety, 152
Sales, 6, 106, 108
Save, 140
Scott, Jerry, 35
Screen, 146
Secondary, 26
Self-education, 6

Serial, 8
Serial I/O, 66, 141
Service, 16, 18, 152, 158
Simulations, 85
Smart, 36
Soft uses, 114
Software, 8, 12, 14, 40, 61, 90, 118, 125
Sound, 42, 149, 154
Special characters, 41
Sports information, 55
Standard keyboard, 42
Star Raiders, 6, 27
Starship, 6
States & Capitals, 82
Stocks and Bonds, 43, 47, 58
Storage, 22, 112
Storage medium, 122
Stores, 17
Student, 49, 90
Super Breakout, 6
Super terminal, 61
Survey, 111
System clock, 133

Teachers, 90
Teaching, 7
Teaching aids, 12
Technical specifications, 150, 156
TeleLink, 61, 62

Teleconferencing, 48, 50
Telephone, 47
Telephone coupler, 142
Television, 47, 121, 146
Terminal, 61, 74
The Source, 52
Time-sharing systems, 75
Toll free number, 6, 45
Touch sensivite keyboard, 21
Turtle Graphics, 81
Tutorial, 85
Tutorial programs, 83

UART, 133
UPI, 54
United Press International, 54
User friendliness, 5, 6, 43, 91, 93, 121, 152, 156

Video display, 19, 41, 115, 140, 146, 154
VisiCalc, 107, 118
Voices, 30
Volatile memory, 139

Window, 108
Word processing, 8, 12, 15, 25, 39, 93, 100, 118
Word processor, 72, 118
Wrap-around, 122

Home Use

This card can serve as a guide to computer buying. We have marked the areas that we feel are most important for home use.

	Education	Entertainment	Programming	Personal Finance	Personal Record keeping	Communication with Computer Services	Word Processing (Letter and manuscript writing)
Video Display							
TV Set	*	*	*	*	*	*	*
Special monitor							
Character display	*		*	*	*	*	*
Screen editing			*				
Color Number of colors	*	*	*				
Background change	*	*	*				
Change text color	*	*	*				
Graphics Text modes	*	*	*				
Total number of graphic modes	*	*	*				
Highest resolution	*	*	*		*	*	*
Additional graphics	*	*	*				
Sound							
Cassette recorder to TV	*	*					
Automatic volume control			*				
Small speaker within computer	*	*	*				
Volume levels							
Number of voices	*	*	*				
Number of different musical notes	*	*	*				
Number of different tonal qualities	*	*	*				
Keyboard							
Upper and lower letter case	*						*
Number of special function keys	*						*
Number of special graphics characters	*	*	*				
Total number of keys			*				
Full-size typewriter-style keyboard			*				*
Pressure-sensitive keyboard							

Home Use

	Education	Entertainment	Programming	Personal Finance	Personal Record Keeping	Communication with Computer Services	Word Processing (Letter and manuscript writing)
Technical Specifications							
Main microprocessor chip							
Custom LSI chips			*	*	*		*
RAM (maximum-minimum)			*	*	*		*
BASIC removable	*	*	*	*	*	*	*
Input/Output ports	*	*	*	*	*	*	*
Expandability — Special interface card required for add accessories	*	*	*	*	*	*	*
Accessories Available							
RS232C port							
Monitor							
Cassette recorder	*	*					
Disk drive			*	*	*		*
Printer			*	*	*		*
Modem						*	
Input accessories	*	*	*				
User Friendliness							
Cartridge programs	*	*					
Protected doomsday keys	*	*	*	*	*	*	*
Safety — TV protection	*	*	*	*	*	*	*
Safety — Protected boards	*	*	*	*	*	*	*
Safety — Accessories added w/o exposure of parts	*	*	*	*	*	*	*
Safety — Memory added w/o exposure of parts	*	*	*	*	*	*	*
Safety — Accessories added with easily identified cables	*	*	*	*	*	*	*
Service							
Manufacturer service centers	*	*	*	*	*	*	*
Servicing dealer network	*	*	*	*	*	*	*
After-Sale Support							
Magazine for owners	*	*	*	*	*	*	*
User group support program	*		*				
Toll-free customer support number	*	*	*	*	*	*	*

Communications Use

This card can serve as a guide to computer buying. We have marked the areas that we feel are most important for communications use.

Video Display

TV Set _____

Special monitor _____

Character display _____ * _____

Screen editing _____

	Number of colors _____
	Background change _____
Color	Change text color _____

	Text modes _____
	Total number of graphic modes _____
Graphics	Highest resolution _____
	Additional graphics _____

Sound

Cassette recorder to TV_____

Automatic volume control _____

Small speaker within computer _____

Volume levels _____

Number of voices _____

Number of different musical notes _____

Number of different tonal qualities_____

Keyboard

Upper and lower letter case _____

Number of special function keys_____

Number of special graphics characters _____

Total number of keys_____

Full-size typewriter-style keyboard _____

Pressure-sensitive keyboard _____

Technical Specifications

Main microprocessor chip _____

Custom LSI chips _____

RAM (maximum-minimum)_____ * _____

BASIC removable _____ * _____

	Input/Output ports_____ * _____
Expand-	Special interface card required
ability	for add accessories _____ * _____

Communications Use

Accessories Available

RS232C port _____

Monitor _____

Cassette recorder _____

Disk drive _____ * _____

Printer _____ * _____

Modem_____ * _____

Input accessories _____

User Friendliness

Cartridge programs _____

Protected doomsday keys_____ * _____

> | TV protection _____
>
> | Protected boards _____ * _____
>
> **Safety** | Accessories added w/o
> exposure of parts _____ * _____
>
> | Memory added w/o exposure
> of parts_____ * _____
>
> | Accessories added with
> easily identified cables _____ * _____

Service

Manufacturer service centers _____ * _____

Servicing dealer network _____ * _____

After-Sale Support

Magazine for owners_____ * _____

User group support program _____ * _____

Toll-free customer support number _____ * _____

Education (Home and School)

This card can serve as a guide to computer buying. We have marked the areas that we feel are most important for educational use.

Video Display

TV Set _____ * _____

Special monitor _____ * _____

Character display _____ * _____

Screen editing _____ * _____

Color

Number of colors _____ * _____

Background change _____ * _____

Change text color _____ * _____

Graphics

Text modes _____ * _____

Total number of graphic modes _____ * _____

Highest resolution _____ * _____

Additional graphics _____ * _____

Sound

Cassette recorder to TV_____ * _____

Automatic volume control _____ * _____

Small speaker within computer ___ * _____

Volume levels _____ * _____

Number of voices _____ * _____

Number of different musical notes _____ * _____

Number of different tonal qualities_____ * _____

Keyboard

Upper and lower letter case _____ * _____

Number of special function keys_____ * _____

Number of special graphics characters _____ * _____

Total number of keys_____ * _____

Full-size typewriter-style keyboard _____

Pressure-sensitive keyboard _____

Technical Specifications

Main microprocessor chip _____

Custom LSI chips _____ * _____

RAM (maximum-minimum)_____ * _____

BASIC removable _____

Expand-ability

Input/Output ports_____ * _____

Special interface card required
for add accessories_____ * _____

Education (Home and School)

Accessories Available

RS232C port _____

Monitor _____

Cassette recorder _____*_____

Disk drive _____

Printer _____

Modem_____

Input accessories _____*_____

User Friendliness

Cartridge programs _____*_____

Protected doomsday keys_____*_____

> TV protection _____*_____
>
> Protected boards _____*_____
>
> Accessories added w/o
> exposure of parts _____*_____
>
> Memory added w/o exposure
> of parts_____*_____
>
> Accessories added with
> easily identified cables _____*_____

Safety

Service

Manufacturer service centers _____*_____

Servicing dealer network _____*_____

After-Sale Support

Magazine for owners_____*_____

User group support program _____*_____

Toll-free customer support number _____*_____

Business and Professional Use

This card can serve as a guide to computer buying. We have marked the areas that we feel are most important for business and professional use.

Video Display

	Word Processing	Financial Analysis	Communications	Graphics and Charts
TV Set				
Special monitor				
Character display	*	*	*	*
Screen editing	*	*	*	*

Color

	Word Processing	Financial Analysis	Communications	Graphics and Charts
Number of colors				*
Background change				*
Change text color				*

Graphics

	Word Processing	Financial Analysis	Communications	Graphics and Charts
Text modes				*
Total number of graphic modes				*
Highest resolution	*	*	*	*
Additional graphics				*

Sound

	Word Processing	Financial Analysis	Communications	Graphics and Charts
Cassette recorder to TV				
Automatic volume control				
Small speaker within computer				
Volume levels				
Number of voices				
Number of different musical notes				
Number of different tonal qualities				

Keyboard

	Word Processing	Financial Analysis	Communications	Graphics and Charts
Upper and lower letter case	*			
Number of special function keys	*	*	*	*
Number of special graphics characters				*
Total number of keys	*	*	*	*
Full-size typewriter-style keyboard	*			
Pressure-sensitive keyboard				

Technical Specifications

	Word Processing	Financial Analysis	Communications	Graphics and Charts
Main microprocessor chip				
Custom LSI chips				

Business and Professional Use

	Word Processing	Financial Analysis	Communications	Graphics and Charts
RAM (maximum-minimum)	*	*	*	*
BASIC removable	*	*	*	*
Expandability — Input/Output ports	*	*	*	*
Expandability — Special interface card required for add accessories	*	*	*	*

Accessories Available

	Word Processing	Financial Analysis	Communications	Graphics and Charts
RS232C port	*		*	
Monitor				
Cassette recorder				
Disk drive	*	*	*	*
Printer	*	*	*	*
Modem				
Input accessories				

User Friendliness

	Word Processing	Financial Analysis	Communications	Graphics and Charts
Cartridge programs				
Protected doomsday keys	*	*	*	*
Safety — TV protection	*	*	*	*
Safety — Protected boards	*	*	*	*
Safety — Accessories added w/o exposure of parts	*	*	*	*
Safety — Memory added w/o exposure of parts	*	*	*	*
Safety — Accessories added with easily identified cables	*	*	*	*

Service

	Word Processing	Financial Analysis	Communications	Graphics and Charts
Manufacturer service centers	*	*	*	*
Servicing dealer network	*	*	*	*

After-Sale Support

	Word Processing	Financial Analysis	Communications	Graphics and Charts
Magazine for owners	*	*	*	*
User group support program	*	*	*	*
Toll-free customer support number	•	•	•	•

Buy a Computer

Visit a retail store that sells home computers. Bring this card and the cards on the following pages that are relevant to your areas of interest. These cards may assist both you and the salesperson in selecting the computer that is right for your needs.

Minimum Requirements and Preferred Key Features

See the cards on the following pages for minimum requirements and preferred key features according to the various areas of interest.

Identify Primary and Secondary Uses:

Primary Use	Secondary Use	LIST SPECIFIC AREAS OF INTEREST
☐	☐	**HOME USE**
☐	☐	Personal Interest _____
☐	☐	Entertainment _____
☐	☐	Personal Finance _____
☐	☐	Personal Recordkeeping _____
☐	☐	Education – Adult _____
☐	☐	Education – Children _____
☐	☐	Word Processing _____
☐	☐	Communications _____
☐	☐	Programming _____
☐	☐	Other _____
		_____
		_____

☐	☐	**EDUCATIONAL USE** (Home and School)
☐	☐	Adult Education _____
☐	☐	Primary Education _____
☐	☐	Secondary Education _____
☐	☐	College Education _____
☐	☐	Computer Instruction _____
☐	☐	Other _____
☐	☐	**COMMUNICATIONS USE**
☐	☐	Home _____
☐	☐	School _____
☐	☐	Business _____
☐	☐	**BUSINESS/PROFESSIONAL USE**
☐	☐	Word Processing _____
☐	☐	Financial Analysis _____
☐	☐	Graphics and Charts _____
☐	☐	Communications _____
☐	☐	Other _____

If you buy an Atari Home Computer, write your name and address below and attach this card to your warranty card and return them together to Atari. Atari will send you a free gift.   Available in U.S. Only.

FREE GIFT OFFER

Name _____

Address _____

City & State _____

Zip Code _____

‖‖‖

BUSINESS REPLY CARD
FIRST CLASS PERMIT NO. 143   BEAVERTON, OREGON

Postage will be paid by addressee

dilithium Press

P.O. Box E
Beaverton, Oregon 97075